A Step-by-Step Guide to a Florida Native Yard

UNIVERSITY PRESS OF FLORIDA

Florida A&M University, Tallahassee
Florida Atlantic University, Boca Raton
Florida Gulf Coast University, Ft. Myers
Florida International University, Miami
Florida State University, Tallahassee
New College of Florida, Sarasota
University of Central Florida, Orlando
University of Florida, Gainesville
University of North Florida, Jacksonville
University of South Florida, Tampa
University of West Florida, Pensacola

A Step-by-Step Guide to a
Florida Native Yard

Ginny Stibolt and Marjorie Shropshire

UNIVERSITY PRESS OF FLORIDA

Gainesville / Tallahassee / Tampa / Boca Raton

Pensacola / Orlando / Miami / Jacksonville / Ft. Myers / Sarasota

Library of Congress Control Number: 2017947645
ISBN 978-0-8130-6463-5

The University Press of Florida is the scholarly publishing agency for
the State University System of Florida, comprising Florida A&M
University, Florida Atlantic University, Florida Gulf Coast University,
Florida International University, Florida State University, New College
of Florida, University of Central Florida, University of Florida, University
of North Florida, University of South Florida, and University of West Florida.

University Press of Florida
15 Northwest 15th Street
Gainesville, FL 32611-2079
http://upress.ufl.edu

We'd like to dedicate this book to the members
of the Florida Native Plant Society, who work hard
to spread the word on the benefits of native landscapes.
Twenty percent of the royalties of this book will be paid
directly to the society to further their mission.

The mission of the Florida Native Plant Society
is to promote the preservation, conservation, and
restoration of the native plants and native plant
communities of Florida.

Contents

Preface

Marjorie attended a symposium where Doug Tallamy was a keynote speaker. After his talk, a woman asked for advice: "I have a small yard filled with exotics. How do I get started?"

Her question sparked an idea that became this book, which has been designed specifically to help answer her question. The main premise is to help her and many others who have similar questions to apply the findings of Tallamy's work in their own small Florida yards.

Marjorie and Ginny have known each other for years and have worked on a number of projects for the Florida Native Plant Society. Ginny recruited Marjorie to be the illustrator for *Organic Methods for Vegetable Gardening in Florida* (2013) and again for *The Art of Maintaining a Florida Native Landscape* (2015). For this book Marjorie is coauthor, since her drawings are central to the content.

This book is also designed to be a companion to *The Art of Maintaining a Florida Native Landscape*; it provides more detailed plans and specific arrangements that people can use in their yards. We assume that you will consult that book for its in-depth information on planting methods and tactics to reduce ongoing maintenance. Also, we suggest several additional references in the Introduction to help you make the best decisions as you move forward with your native landscaping.

We wish to thank David Chiapinni and many other people we have worked with over the years for sharing their knowledge and their experience. We also wish to thank Steve Turnipseed and Troy Springer for their thorough reading of the manuscript. Also, we'd like to thank the talented staff at University Press of Florida for working with us on this project.

Happy nativizing!

Ginny Stibolt (www.GreenGardeningMatters.com)
Marjorie Shropshire (www.Sharkrivercreative.com)

NOTE

Dr. Tallamy, an entomology professor at the University of Delaware, published *Bringing Nature Home: How You Can Sustain Wildlife with Native Plants* in 2007, which has provided scientific proof and credible arguments for why natives are important, even in small landscapes. Since then he has been in great demand as a speaker all over the country.

A Step-by-Step Guide to a
Florida Native Yard

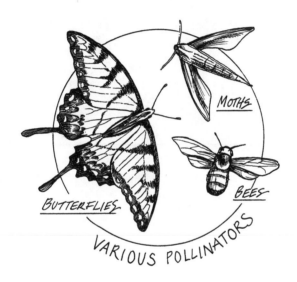

MOTHS

BUTTERFLIES

BEES

VARIOUS POLLINATORS

Introduction

The costs of increasing the percentage and biomass of natives in our suburban landscapes are small, and the benefits are immense. Increasing the percentage of natives in suburbia is a grassroots solution to the extinction crisis. . . . We can each make a measurable difference almost immediately by planting a native nearby. As gardeners and stewards of our land, we have never been so empowered—and the ecological stakes have never been so high.

—*Doug Tallamy*

Many Floridians are adding more Florida native plants to their landscapes. The reasons for this trend vary widely:

- To reduce maintenance costs—both time and money
- To reduce irrigation and water use
- To reduce pollution and runoff for the sake of nearby waterways
- To attract birds
- To use fewer pesticides—organic or not—for health reasons
- To save monarch butterflies and other pollinators
- To reduce utility bills by cooling the air and shading south or western exposures
- To reduce frustrations with dealing with poor turf grass condition
- To create an authentic Florida yard

"How do I get started with a more native landscape?" is the question many people are asking. Most of Florida's urban and suburban landscapes are dominated by acres of lawn that are typically overfertilized, overwatered, and regularly sprayed with herbicides, insecticides, and fungicides. In addition, lawns are often not allowed to go dormant and are overseeded with cool-weather grass to keep them bright green in the winter. Planting beds around the lawns are often filled with thirsty exotic plants that are replaced each season. Landscapes are frequently outlined by

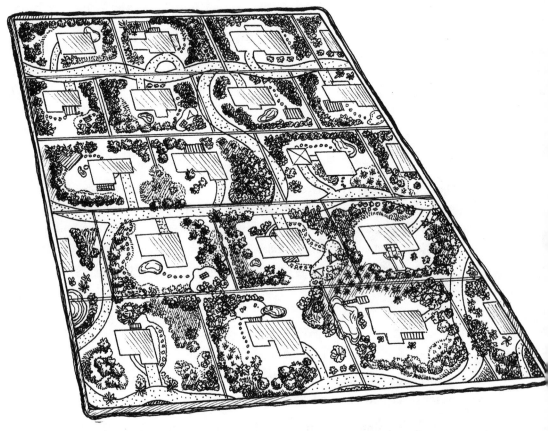

WHEN A NEIGHBORHOOD GOES NATIVE, IT WELCOMES
BIRDS, BUTTERFLIES, AND OTHER WILDLIFE.

monoculture and monolithic hedges of exotic plants (often full-sized trees) that are severely trimmed. Many yards feature plants that are invasive in Florida, and surprisingly, as bad as these plants are for Florida's natural areas, garden centers still sell them and neighbors who don't realize that these plants are harmful to Florida's natural habitats still share them.

This book takes a step-by-step approach to creating a more native landscape in one small urban or suburban yard. Our sample yard is 100' by 145' (about one-third of an acre), which is typical of many Florida yards. There are many ways to approach native landscaping, and several real-life vignettes have been included throughout the text to demonstrate other approaches and methods to fit specific situations. These describe how real people handled their problems to end up with beautiful, mostly native landscapes.

So let's get started!

CREATING HABITAT

Humans have altered most of the land in the lower forty-eight states and have con-verted over 62,500 square miles to lawns, according to Doug Tallamy's seminal book *Bringing Nature Home: How You Can Sustain Wildlife with Native Plants* (2007). An aerial view of the flyway migrating songbirds use over urban and suburban Tampa shows an area nearly devoid of trees. There are more than 6,300 square miles of lawn in Florida, making lawns the largest acreage crop in the Sunshine State. This equals about one-tenth of all the lawns in the lower 48 states. What has this done to our wildlife?

The Audubon Society, which has been counting birds for more than 100 years, has documented the population slumps in most of Florida's bird species. Audubon says that loss of habitat is by far the biggest reason for the populations of birds, but humans and their civilization have caused even further damage.

Since birds have been so diligently watched that they can serve as our "canaries in the coal mine" in Florida's ecosystems. The decline of native birds is indicative of a general decline in most of Florida's native fauna, from butterflies and lightning bugs to panthers and otters. A variety of statewide environmental groups are working to restore more of "the real Florida" on a large scale. (See Resources below for a list of some of these organizations.)

In addition to supporting these environmental groups, you can also make a real

Some Florida birds in peril (populations from 1968 to 2012)

Species	Annual % change for 44 years	Notes
American woodcock	-0.91	Winters in Florida. Needs grassy meadow areas in open woodlands.
Red-cockaded woodpecker	-3.09	Nests in mature trees, mostly longleaf pines.
Brown thrasher	-1.06	Thrives at edges of wooded areas in shrubs and small trees.
Bachman's sparrow	-3.04	Hides in dense ground cover such as palmettos and wire grass in open forests.
Eastern meadowlark	-3.21	A year-round resident of open meadows.

Note: If you start with 1,000,000 birds and the population is reduced by 3 percent per year, at the end of twenty years, nearly half of the birds (474,370) will have been lost.

difference by changing your urban or suburban yard to include more groups of native plants in butterfly gardens, rain gardens, meadows, and/or small groves of trees and shrubs. While it may seem that changes made to one yard are too insignificant to help, Tallamy has shown that individual lots populated by groupings of native plants really do make a difference.

The positive effects on wildlife populations will be greatly enhanced when habitat in your suburban yard combines with other native yards in your neighborhood, open community lands, church properties, and schoolyards that have been planted with native plants. The combined properties create corridors of food and shelter that are useful to many types of wildlife. Each property that goes native is another "green" square in the region's habitat tapestry, and the greater the percentage of green, the more likely it is that wildlife, from migratory and local birds to butterflies and other pollinators, can successfully complete their life cycles.

CERTIFIED HABITAT

The National Wildlife Federation (NWF) has been running a backyard wildlife habitat certification program since 1973. The number of certified habitats across the country approaches one million as this book is being written. The NWF lists several criteria for creating certified habitat and provides good guidelines for transforming a landscape into one that provides more ecosystem services, whether it's a yard, a schoolyard, a churchyard, or community-owned property.
Here are some of the NWF's suggestions:

Provide Shelter and Places for Wildlife to Raise Their Young

Vary the type of vegetation so you have some areas that will be kept as meadows with bunching grasses and wildflowers, and don't be quick about cutting back spent flower heads. Plant shrubs and trees in groves or thickets so birds and butterflies can find shelter, and include a stick pile in a back corner for cover. Snags (dead trees) add to the shelter options. Of course, you can also add manmade houses for birds, bats, and native bees to your landscape to add instant shelter and visual appeal.

Provide Food Sources

Many people add bird feeders in their landscapes. These may benefit birds as long as you are a consistent resource for them. A feeder will change the mix of the bird species that populate your yard. Feeders are probably not necessary if you have a wide variety of plants that bear fruit, nuts, nectar, and pollen. In addition to flowers, butterfly gardens should also include host plants that will be eaten by their larvae. Ideas for designing butterfly gardens are covered in Step 5.

Control Domestic Cats

Cats act as subsidized predators in the landscape and have been shown to kill and harass birds, lizards, and other wildlife. Keep them inside for their own safety and to help your yard become a working ecosystem. Audubon research estimates that domestic cats kill 2.4 billion birds in the United States. The number killed annually from other causes pales in comparison: 589 million die when they hit buildings, 289 million die when they are hit by cars, and 25 million are killed when they hit power lines. Cats cause almost three times more bird kills than the total of the next three causes of human-related bird deaths, but it could be the easiest one to remedy.

Add Water Features

Having clean, accessible water helps a wide variety of wildlife. While a birdbath or container water garden is okay and certainly better than nothing, these small water features will be more useful to wildlife and add more visual appeal in the landscape if you add a solar-powered pump with a trickle fountain.

A pond, even a small, preformed one, offers many more ecosystem services because it can host fish, frogs, and dragonflies. If you can arrange for a small mud beach at one edge of the pond, then butterflies, mud daubers, and other insects will have a supply of wet soil to use. A pond also provides a damp habitat for a different set of native plants that might not survive in your yard otherwise. Mosquitoes can be limited by adding mosquito fish that are native to Florida to the pond. Dragonfly larvae will also eat the mosquito larvae. Keep in mind that a pond, even a small one, will attract wading birds, so make sure the fish and frogs have places to hide. It's a good sign when wading birds can find their own niche in your yard's ecosystem. See more on ponds in Step 2.

Retain Stormwater

When homeowners build rain gardens and use rain barrels as part of their landscaping, it reduces flow of stormwater over streets and driveways on its way to storm drains. This in turn reduces pollution of nearby waterways. This is just one of the many sustainable gardening ideas suggested for landscapes that are more wildlife friendly. For more information, see Step 2.

Overcome the Poison Cycle

In order to build a wildlife-friendly landscape filled with butterflies and birds, stop all landscape-wide pesticides (organic or otherwise) including those used by many lawn-care companies. A soil ecosystem beneath a lawn that has been poisoned and fertilized on a regular basis will need some time to adjust after these applications

ATTRACT INSECTS - AND BIRDS, TO YOUR YARD

stop. When the soil's microbes and macrobes recover, it will be able to support plants without the help of synthetic fertilizers. If you will be replacing some of a treated lawn with native plants, it may be best to let the area go through a recovery period for a few months. You can hasten the soil's recovery by applying a light top dressing of compost. While the compost will add some nutrients, its microbes are more important in the rehabilitation of a soil's ecosystem. Keep in mind that compost can wash off in a heavy rain and add to pollution of nearby waterways. It's best to apply it when heavy rains are not expected. Also, compost does the most for the soil and for plants when it's applied in early spring, when grass and many other plants are coming out of dormancy in Florida.

If you want birds in your yard, you must first invite the bugs. It's a vital step for successful ecosystem gardening. In a balanced ecosystem, predators will be in the minority. In other words, in a natural environment, there are many more bugs to create a continuous food supply for the predators—birds, dragonflies, bats, lizards, and others.

Create Some Low-Traffic Areas

In addition to the conditions listed above, the best wildlife habitat will be in areas that are not in constant use by humans or pets. On the other hand, people, especially children, will have more interest in habitat creation if they can see the birds and butterflies including their caterpillars up close. It's a balance.

PUBLIC PERCEPTION

While the overall public reaction to native landscapes is positive, sometimes community associations and municipalities have strict rules so that everyone will have similar-looking landscapes. These usually consist of mostly lawn with only a fringe of other plants. In this type of situation, the controlling organizations may balk at a reduced-lawn or no-lawn landscape. They may not consider freedom lawns—lawns that are free from pesticides, fertilizers, overseeding in winter, and overwatering—to be acceptable either.

Learn if there are regulations before you start your native landscaping and proceed within their limits. Most of these regulations have been written so the neighborhood will look cared for and to maintain property values. Most people who live in controlled neighborhoods and who have been successful in transforming their yards from mostly lawn to mostly natives have worked with neighborhood organizations by politely presenting their plans and ensuring that the end results will look "nice." Even if you feel that the regulations are unfair or that people are getting upset over nothing, being patient and polite is almost always more effective than getting angry. If you are looking to change the rules, another option is to run for the controlling board and work from the inside—a "no-grass roots" maneuver.

The "Florida-Friendly Landscaping" statute, which was passed in 2009, states, "A deed restriction or covenant or local government ordinance may not prohibit or be enforced so as to prohibit any property owner from implementing Florida-friendly landscaping on their land or create any conflicting requirement." This law was designed to improve Florida's waterways by encouraging people to reduce their use of fertilizers and pesticides. There are many resources and articles about this topic on the University of Florida's Florida-Friendly Landscaping website (http://fyn.ifas.ufl.edu).

To help you make a case for native landscapes and to demonstrate how attractive they can be, a PowerPoint slide show created for this book, called "Why Native Landscapes Are Important" is available at no cost on the Florida Native Plant Society website (www.FNPS.org) in the resources section. The slides in this presentation are self-explanatory and a narrative text is provided, so you don't need any special training to run this presentation. You'll probably also wish to talk about your own plans and about some of the specific reasons native plants could enhance the neighborhood. Maybe add some ideas for a butterfly garden on community property or in a local schoolyard so that everyone wins. Who wouldn't want a butterfly garden? Grants for community wildflower projects are available from the Florida Wildflower Foundation (www.flawildflowers.org). Getting the community involved in such a group project may pave the way for an easing of landscaping restrictions and may encourage other people in the neighborhood to follow your lead.

Whether you live where there are formal landscaping regulations or not, you can reduce objections or questions from neighbors by working to keep your landscape neat. What looks like a butterfly-friendly meadow to you may look like a bunch of weeds to someone who keeps a greener-than-green lawn punctuated by shrubs and trees that have been trimmed into gumdrop or lollypop shapes. You can combat the perception of weediness by surrounding meadow areas with trimmed native hedges or rows of bunching grasses. Such edges keep a landscape's appearance tidy. You could also create a path through the area that leads to a bench under a tree or a pergola. Paths or other outdoor features let people know that you planned the landscape.

The plans included in this book include tidy edge plantings for this reason. Even if the edge is temporary for only a couple of years while plants mature, it's still worth the effort. If you know the border plants are temporary, use ones that are inexpensive or easy to transplant. You could also use large planters that can be moved as your landscape needs change.

Some people change their landscapes a little at a time. This tends to be more acceptable in fussy neighborhoods and is certainly more affordable. But a more dramatic changeover can also be accomplished without too much complaint if neighbors know what the plan is. This book assumes a relatively gradual process.

However you proceed in creating a more native landscape, it's a good idea to educate passersby what you are doing with small signs indicating that your yard is now an authentic Florida garden, a certified habitat, a butterfly haven, or a kid-safe, poison-free zone. Your actions may encourage your neighbors to rethink the poisonous landscape warning signs that their yard service people install after each treatment. Maybe they would like to have a kid-safe zone and add native plants to their yards so their kids can watch butterflies, too. The more neighbors you can recruit to stop pesticides and to install native plants, the better the result will be in creating a habitat corridor in your neighborhood.

MULCH AND COMPOST

Using a plant-based mulch around your newly planted trees, shrubs, and herbaceous plants is highly recommended because it provides several benefits:

- It reduces weed growth, especially when it is first applied to bare soil.
- It helps retain soil moisture.
- It moderates temperature fluctuations.
- It eventually turns into a rich soil. Mulching is also called sheet composting.

The layer of mulch should be between two and four inches thick, but it should not touch the plants, especially around the trunks of your trees or shrubs. It's best not to lay cardboard, newspaper, or weed cloth under the mulch. You will probably need to reapply the mulch every second year until your trees and shrubs are providing enough leaf drop to be self-mulching.

That being said, an extensive mulch cover that is merely punctuated with a few specimen plants should not be the ultimate goal of a nonlawn landscape. Wide areas of mulch are not particularly attractive and every rogue weed will stand out like a sore thumb. This often happens in commercially maintained landscapes because mulching an area is quick and easy. Also, when you plant for tomorrow—not today—there are wide spaces between young trees and shrubs.

To combat the sea of mulch landscape while trees and shrubs are maturing, use filler plants, container gardens, and/or ground covers between them. Use mulch around plants, but it should not be a dominant element in the landscape. A few weeds growing among a group of wildflowers might be hardly noticeable, but noxious weeds should be pulled before they get too large or release seeds. The timing of the weeding sessions in the wildflowers will be more flexible than they are for the more obvious weeds growing alone in the mulch.

Types of Mulch

Plant-Based Mulches

There are a number of commonly used plant-based mulches. They include leaves from trees and shrubs, chipped wood from arborists, pine bark nuggets, pine needles (sometimes called pine straw), straw, sawdust, and shredded wood—probably the most commonly purchased mulch. Some of these mulches are free and local, such as the leaves and pine needles that fall on your property and on neighborhood roads. Some people even ask neighbors for their raked leaves and yard debris. The supply of these items tends to be seasonal, so you can store the excess in a pile until needed.

Arborists that come in to remove trees often bring wood-chipping machines. If you hear a wood chipper working in your area, you can ask for the load of chips. Most arborists will gladly dump them on your property to save a trip to the landfill and to avoid the dumping fee. You can also call local arborists to let them know that you would be willing to take their next load. At some landfills, county residents can dig out mulch or compost created from yard waste collection programs or from arborists' chipped wood piles. The quality will vary depending on the location and the time of year.

If you need to purchase a mulch for your planting project, please don't buy unsustainable cypress mulch because whole cypress forests are being shredded to feed

our mulching habit. Use one that is a by-product of another process or one that is manufactured using shredded invasive trees such as paperbark (*Melaleuca quin-quenervia*), which is sold under the name FloriMulch.

Gravel

Using gravel as a mulch substitute is not recommended for most landscapes in Florida because the annual 50 inches of rainfall provides enough moisture for abundant weed growth through the gravel and leaves will gather on top of the gravel that will need to be removed. Florida is not a desert and the rock- and gravel-based xeriscaping that can work well in much drier habitats will end up becoming messy. That being said, gravel could be useful as a base under tightly spaced stepping-stones or pavers and gravel is useful in fire-wise landscapes.

Rubber

Rubber mulch sounds like a sustainable idea (reusing old tires), but it has been shown to leach poisonous compounds into the soil as it breaks down, it is not effective in keeping weeds down, and it does nothing to help build better soil. In addition, rubber mulch is highly flammable.

Compost

Compost is rather ineffective as a mulch when it comes to reducing weeds or holding in moisture, but it will enhance the underlying soil. For purposes of this book, compost is defined as local plant matter that has decomposed so that it no longer looks like the original plants. (See below for resources on building compost.)

For compost to work best for native landscaping needs, no enhancements should be added. Many people add the manure of herbivores (chickens, rabbits, horses, or cows) or synthetic fertilizers to compost they use on their vegetable gardens to enhance the nutrients for fast crop growth, but don't use this for native plants. The high nitrogen content of these manures could push the natives into unsustainable growth spurts. The goal of native landscaping is to approximate a natural environment so that after initial care, the plants will be able to survive for the long run without too much assistance.

Uses for Compost in the Landscape

- As a top dressing outside the area of the planting hole for trees and shrubs to entice their roots to grow outward. See Step 3 for more details.
- As a major component in the soil mix for container gardens and later as a top dressing in a long-term container garden to keep the soil microbes refreshed.
- As an enriching amendment for a whole area whether the soil is sand or clay.

Quick Compost Recipe

Purchase organic soil mix (no synthetic fertilizers and no moisture beads) in bags. Empty the bags onto bare soil just before it rains or dampen it with rain-barrel water (or two-day-old city water so that the chlorine and other volatile chemicals will have evaporated). If you have some dead leaves, lay leaves on the soil first and then alternate layers of soil mix and leaves. Keep it damp, and in just a couple of weeks, microbes and larger critters like worms and centipedes will have begun to work in the soil. You can then use it as a compost top dressing to condition soil.

EDUCATE YOURSELF

Many people who move to Florida from other regions of the country are surprised at how different gardening is here with our seven-month dry season and five-month wet season. Our soil never freezes, even in the northern regions of the state. All of these conditions change the plant palette and general gardening strategies. So don't try to recreate a New England or Mid-Atlantic landscape here in Florida. At the other extreme, some people new to Florida gardening make the mistake of adding too many exotic tropicals north of planting zone 11, where they need to be protected from frosts. Also, the tropical plants may make their yards look more like Hawaii than Florida.

> *Native plants are the best suited to our climate and are most likely to succeed, plus they become part of the local ecosystem.*

Before embarking on converting your landscape, you'll need to know what you have and what would be the best natives for your particular situation and location. The possibilities are endless, but choosing plants that are most likely to succeed will make the project easier and more satisfying. While it's good to invest in some Florida gardening books for ongoing reference, the quickest way to assess the existing plants is to bring in experts, and if you have more than a few mature trees, one of the experts should be a certified arborist. Go to the Trees Are Good website (www.treesaregood.com) to find local arborists.

Also, it's important to get out into the "real Florida" by taking guided tours at local state parks and going on field trips with your local Florida Native Plant Society (FNPS) chapter or other outdoors groups. Removing invasive plants on local workdays will help you recognize them at all stages and add to your knowledge of how much damage they can do in our natural areas and the best ways to get rid of them. Taking a master naturalist course will provide a deeper understanding of local ecosystems. Attending conferences, workshops, symposiums, and monthly meetings of organizations that bring in expert speakers will also add to your knowledge. When you participate in these activities, you'll also find people dedicated to Florida and her natural areas. They may become important contacts for further research as you proceed with nativizing your landscape.

VEGETABLE GARDENS

While adding an edible garden plot to the landscape is a great idea, this book does not cover vegetable gardening. Please use *Organic Methods for Vegetable Gardening in Florida*, by Ginny Stibolt and Melissa Contreras (Gainesville: University Press of Florida, 2013) for details on how to grow edibles successfully in Florida. Again, no matter how many vegetables you grew in another region of the country, you will find that Florida gardening is definitely different.

Definitions of Native, Exotic, and Invasive

NATIVE

A plant that was known to a region before European settlers disrupted the landscape —approximately 500 years ago. The authority on nativeness used for this book is the Atlas of Florida Plants (http://florida.plantatlas.usf.edu/).

REGIONAL NATIVE

A plant that is native to one part of the state but is planted outside its native range. For instance, the Eastern purple coneflower (*Echinacea purpurea*) is native to only one county in the Florida (Gadsden County in the Panhandle) but is sold in all of northern Florida. It would be a regional native in Jacksonville.

EXOTIC OR NONNATIVE

A plant that is native to a different region or different part of the world has been introduced here, either on purpose or accidentally.

INVASIVE

An exotic plant that has damaged natural habitats by replacing natives in those ecosystems. The Florida Exotic Pest Plant Council (FLEPPC; www.FLEPPC.org) keeps two lists of exotic plants invasive to Florida: Category I, which lists plants known to have done the most damage; and Category II, which lists plants which have done less damage but have the potential to do more if left uncontrolled. Most exotics are not invasive.

AGGRESSIVE

Many natives are aggressive in urban and suburban landscapes but are not invasive by definition. For instance, Spanish needle (*Bidens alba*) is a native plant that will take over any open or disturbed area. An aggressive exotic plant, whether it's on a FLEPPC list or not, should be avoided.

Many plant species have wide ranges, but you'll have much better success if you purchase plants and seeds that are bred from Florida stock. For instance, red maple (*Acer rubrum*) is native to most of Florida, but its native range extends northward to the eastern provinces in Canada. A red maple from Canadian stock would not do well in Florida: it would bloom too late and its leaves would be shed too early in the fall and emerge too late in the spring. Also, it might not do well in our seven-month dry season.

FOR FURTHER REFERENCE

Recommended books and online resources for more background on plants and best practices in landscaping

Resources on Plants

Online

- The Florida Native Plant Society (FNPS; http://fnps.org) has chapters all over the state. You'll learn a lot by attending meetings and going on field trips. Also, the FNPS website has a useful tool where you can generate a list of natives recommended for your county. (20 percent of the royalties for this book will be paid directly to FNPS.)
- The Florida Wildflower Foundation (http://flawildflowers.org) holds an annual symposium and works on many programs to promote more use of Florida's wildflowers across the state. This organization also offers small grants to communities and organizations to cover some of the expenses for seeds, plants, and other ongoing costs of installing wildflower gardens.
- The Florida Wildflowers Growers Cooperative (http://www.floridawildflowers.com) offers seeds of Florida native wildflowers bred from Florida stock.
- The Florida Association of Native Nurseries (http://plantrealflorida.org) is a group of nurseries around the state that actively promote and sell native plants. You can find a local nursery or a specific native plant on their website.
- The Institute for Regional Conservation (http://www.regionalconservation.org) provides a similar service for South Florida called "Natives for your Neighborhood."
- The Florida Exotic Plant Pest Council (http://www.fleppc.org) maintains a website with the list of plants shown to be invasive in Florida's natural areas and information to help you identify those plants.
- The Atlas of Florida Plants (http://florida.plantatlas.usf.edu) provides a list of all of Florida's plants with a range map of the counties where each plant is found—or at least vouchered. (A plant is vouchered when someone has collected and prepared it for storage in a herbarium with its exact location for future reference.) Details include whether plants are native, nonnative, or invasive. A collection of photos is provided for most plants, which can help with identification. (This is the authority used in this book on the native status of plants.)

Books

- Craig Huegel, *Native Florida Plants for Shady Landscapes* (Gainesville: University Press of Florida, 2015). In Florida, we strive to build more shade, but all shade is not equal. This book helps you find plants that thrive in the various types of shade.
- Craig Huegel, *Native Wildflowers and Other Ground Covers for Florida Landscapes* (Gainesville: University Press of Florida, 2012).
- Gil Nelson, *Florida's Best Native Landscape Plants: 200 Readily Available Species for Homeowners and Professionals* (Gainesville: University Press of Florida, 2003). This book provides information about commonly available landscape native plants, including mature size, where to plant, and good companion plants.

Resources on Gardening

Online

- Your local county agricultural extension office may be able to help with plant identifications and general gardening help. Some counties run day-long symposia on various topics, such as building rain barrels. The Institute of Food and Agricultural Services Extension (http://sfyl.ifas.ufl.edu/map/index.shtml) provides a list of offices for the state. The offices may or may not have much specific information on Florida natives, although they do have information on the Florida-Friendly Landscaping program (http://ffl.ifas.ufl.edu/index.html), which includes online resources with sustainable landscaping ideas
- Linda Chalker-Scott's Horticulture Myths website (www.informed-gardener.com) offers scientifically accurate evaluations of horticultural techniques. If you have questions from compost tea to best planting techniques, reading this site will save you time and effort in the long run.

Books

- Ginny Stibolt, *Sustainable Gardening for Florida* (Gainesville: University Press of Florida, 2009). This book provides details and ideas for being a successful gardener in Florida. It includes chapters on composting, rain gardens, and rain barrels.
- Ginny Stibolt, *The Art of Maintaining a Florida Native Landscape* (Gainesville: University Press of Florida, 2015). This book helps people plan for the ongoing maintenance of mostly native landscapes. The no-care landscape is a myth.

Resources on Wildlife and Building Habitat

Online

- The National Wildlife Federation (http://www.nwf.org) offers many ideas for making your landscape wildlife friendly and provides instructions for backyard habitat certification.
- The Audubon Society (http://www.audubon.org) provides information about habitat for birds. The Florida branch of Audubon (http://fl.audubon.org) includes information and activities for Florida.
- The Cornell Lab of Ornithology's YardMap program (http://content.yard-map.org) encourages people to create better habitat for birds in their yards. Its website provides many articles and resources.
- The Butterflies and Moths of North America website (http://www.butterfliesandmoths.org/) will help you identify butterflies and moths. It also provides information about known host and nectar plants for each species.

Books

- Jaret Daniels, *Your Florida Guide to Butterfly Gardening: A Guide for the Deep South* (Gainesville: University Press of Florida, 2000). A good overview of how to create and maintain a butterfly garden.
- Roger Hammer, *Attracting Hummingbirds and Butterflies in Tropical Florida: A Companion for Gardeners* (Gainesville: University Press of Florida, 2015). South Florida gardeners will find useful in this book about creating habitat in their tropical climate.
- Craig Huegel, *Native Plant Landscaping for Wildlife for Florida Wildlife* (Gainesville: University Press of Florida, 2010). This book includes suggestions for attracting wildlife and details on plants that serve this purpose.
- Marc C. Minno and Maria Minno, *Florida Butterfly Gardening: A Complete Guide to Attracting, Identifying, and Enjoying Butterflies* (Gainesville: University Press of Florida, 1999). A Florida classic.
- Marc Minno, Jerry Butler, and Donald Hall (*Florida Butterfly Caterpillars and Their Host Plants* (Gainesville: University Press of Florida, 2005). Useful information about attracting butterflies and growing the plants that host their larvae.
- Doug Tallamy, *Bringing Nature Home: How You Can Sustain Wildlife with Native Plants* (Portland, Ore.: Timber Press, 2009). Tallamy makes the case that planting natives in urban and suburban yards makes a big difference to wildlife, from butterflies to birds.

STEP 1

Assess Your Property

Once you decide to transform your landscape to have less lawn, more native plants, and more sustainable upkeep, it may be tempting to just start ripping out lawn and planting natives. But an overall assessment of your property and a basic plan will help you make better choices, which will help this project progress more smoothly. In the long run, a plan will save you time and money.

KEEP A LANDSCAPING LOG

Designate a notebook or garden book to record information about your landscaping projects. Fill it with sketches, ideas, and notes. One of the most important uses is to keep track of your plant purchases. Keep it small enough that it will be easy to take it with you on educational field trips or shopping excursions to plant sales or native nurseries. A small camera or photo-taking phone will also be useful for recording a plant or landscape you like. To remind you which plant is which, also take a photo of the identification tags. Instead of a paper log, you could also use a tablet computer, which could be set up with a folder and subfolders for various aspects of your landscape projects. These folders could be sequential by year or they could be arranged by topic, like plant purchases or irrigation schedules.

While there are several ways to approach this record keeping, don't skip this step thinking that you'll remember everything: you won't. Another point to remember is that people learn and absorb ideas in different ways and it's been shown that when you process the information in more than one way, you will understand your ideas more fully. Even taking photos helps you "see" a situation better as you compose the photos and then again as you view them.

MASTER SKETCH

A critical step in your planning and record keeping is to create a master sketch of your whole property to follow during your planning and planting process. Ideally, you'd start with some copies of the surveyors' plat, which would be drawn to scale. You could also pace off the edges of your property and the edges of your buildings to approximate the dimensions. Some people find success by printing out a screenshot of a satellite image of their properties on the Internet and then tracing the lines of the edges of your property and of the buildings. Another advantage of a satellite image is that you can see the vegetation of the whole neighborhood

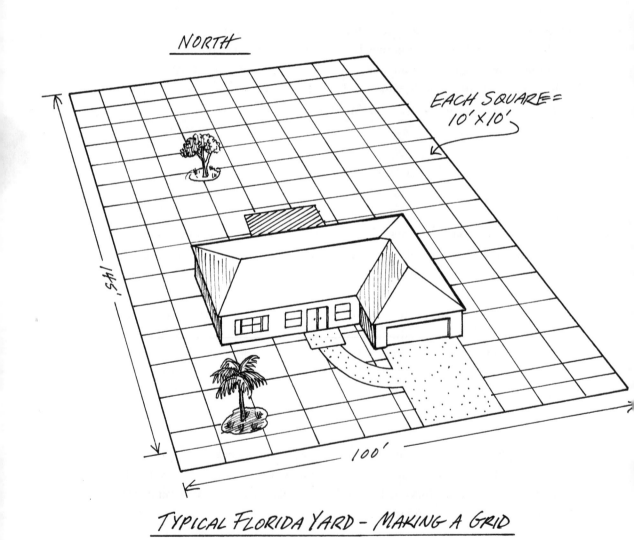

TYPICAL FLORIDA YARD - MAKING A GRID

even if parts of it are hidden behind hedges or buildings. You can save the screen capture to your computer and then bring that file to a copy shop, which can make several enlarged copies for you to use for this project. At the end of this section, there is an empty grid for you to use if you choose.

After you have a grid that includes your property lines, your house, outbuildings such as toolsheds, and hardscape features, fill in the infrastructure details.

Orientation and Infrastructure

Determine the orientation of the buildings and mark "North" on your master sketch. In addition, spend some time watching where and how the sun and shade fall during the day and in different seasons. We all know that the sun is higher in the sky during the summer and that when it's farther south in the sky during winter there are longer shadows. But in this exercise, note the type of shade and how far into your landscape it falls. Shade from deciduous trees will be dense in the summer but partly sunny in the winter. You'll want to know how long those deciduous trees are bare, because in Florida, it may only be a month or two depending on the tree species and your planting zone. In South Florida, deciduous trees will have less impact in your landscape.

Shade cast by buildings and other structures is solid, and on the north side there will be areas that might not receive any direct sun. Figure out how far out shade from buildings is in the winter and compare that with the shadows formed in the summer. Mark the shade characteristics on this initial sketch.

Note overhead wires and locate the underground infrastructure on your sketch such as irrigation pipes, septic systems or sewer pipes, electrical wiring, and French drains. If you don't know where your underground pipes and conduits are, call 811 to connect to a local coordination center that will contact all the utility services with underground service in your area or go to the Sunshine 811 website (http://www.sunshine811.com/) to start the procedure. It will take at least two business days for representatives from all the local utilities to visit your property and mark where their pipes are. This is a free service.

In addition to utilities, there may be French drains to handle downspout water and the underground pipes and switches for a built-in irrigation system. You can usually find the irrigation contractor's contact information at the system's control center, but if that's missing, ask around the neighborhood to find some names of local irrigation contractors. Call the contractors and ask if someone can come out with a metal detector to locate the underground switches and help you figure out the approximate locations of pipes based on the switch locations and the sprinkler heads. Expect to pay for this service, but it will be much less expensive in the long run to know where not to plant large trees. This is also a good opportunity for the contractor to check how well the irrigation system is working and whether you need to replace sprinkler heads. Also have the contractor check the flowing pressure of at least one of the irrigation heads in each zone and watch the master meter to confirm that there are no leaks.

After you have marked all the infrastructure locations, indicate their locations on your master sketch. Make sure that your landscaping plans don't infringe on these structures. Keep in mind that some trees have more aggressive roots than others and that many septic tanks and sewer pipes have been defeated by water-seeking roots. The roots of an average tree reach well beyond its drip line (where water

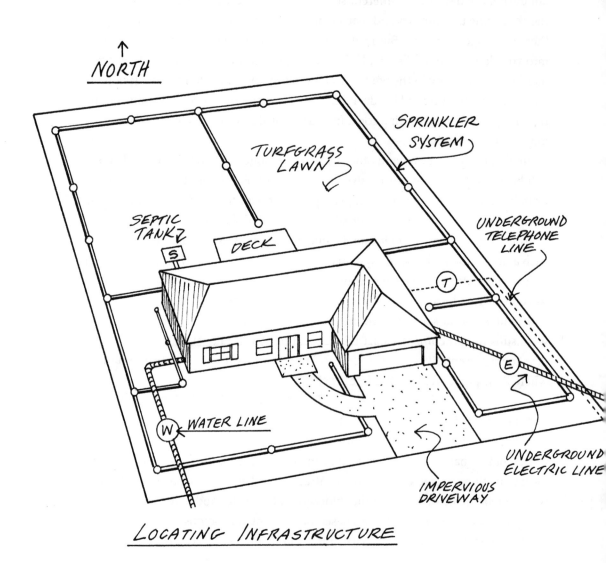

LOCATING INFRASTRUCTURE

dripping from the tips of the branches would fall). If the drip line is ten feet from the trunk, the surface roots could extend to thirty feet or more. Be sure to ask about the aggressiveness of the roots when choosing trees. Some trees, such as willows and maples, are known for having aggressive, water-seeking roots. If you want trees in areas near pipes, cement driveways, foundations, and other hardscape features, consider using palms. Palms do not produce wood with annual rings like true trees and their roots do not expand. Tree root expansion is what causes the cracking or dislodging of hard infrastructure features.

After the infrastructure is marked on your plan, the next step is to evaluate the soil and the plants.

Determine the Wet and Dry Spots in Your Landscape

There may be low places that stay wet or moist after a rain. If a spot is habitually wet, moisture-loving plants such as mosses, rushes, and ferns may already be growing there, even if the area has been managed as a lawn, so be sure to look for them. Some of the wet spots may be artificially produced from over-irrigation or from irrigation system leaks, so be aware of that.

A sandy location will dry out quickly after a storm, but clay soil or rock substrate may hold water for days. It's possible that you could have more than one type of soil in different locations even on a small property because of natural transitions or because changes that were made when your house was built.

It's just as important to know the really dry spots in your landscape so you can plant only drought-tolerant gardens there. Signs of this may be dead spots in your lawn, reduced sizes in rows of plants, wilting plants, or dieback in trees or shrubs.

Test the Soil

Take samples in several places. Even on a small lot, there could be different soil types. Some may become obvious as you look for wet and dry areas, but some of the soil differences may be subtler. You may have different soils on your property because of materials a builder or developer imported. Another reason for different soil types is the fact that plants such as pine trees acidify soil near them. A natural transition in the original ecosystem could also cause different soil types. For instance, if your property backs up to a natural body of water, there may be more clay in the soil from that part of your property. Soil on the lee side of a building, which regularly receives salt spray, will be less salty.

The local extension office has sample boxes and data sheets that explain the soil sampling procedures. Keep in mind that most of their information is for farmers, so be sure to ask for details on home soil testing. It will take a couple of weeks to get the results, but then you'll know about the nutrient levels and acidity (pH) of the soil on your property. This is important to know so that you can choose the best plants for the soil you have.

The most sustainable approach is not to attempt to alter the soil chemistry to accommodate special plants, because those plants will be unlikely to thrive no matter how much you try to match the soil to their needs. It will become an endless and potentially expensive cycle of adding things to that soil. The one exception to this is growing edible crops, which generally require a much richer soil than our native Florida soils to produce fast growth and good yields.

Decide Which Plants to Keep and Which to Eliminate

Identify the plants you have and then decide which ones to keep (at least temporarily) and which ones have to be removed. Mark this on your master sketch so you'll have a feel for new spaces that will be available.

If you're new to Florida, there is·so much to learn it can be overwhelming, even for people who are longtime gardeners in other climates. You can start by using a selection of the books and online resources mentioned in the introduction to this book.

The local agricultural extension office can help with plant identification when you're stuck. If possible, take them a branch of a plant with a flower or fruit to provide them with enough information to identify it. A photo of the whole plant can be useful, too. Plants are classified by their flowers and fruit, so a sprig with leaves alone may not provide enough information for an accurate identification. As mentioned in the introduction, members of your local native plant society chapter or local master gardeners may also be able to help you learn to identify your natives and other plants.

If you're lucky, there will be some well-established natives growing in appropriate places on your lot. But if your property was cleared and landscaped by the developer who bought whatever was cheap and available in bulk or by former owners who bought plants from big-box stores, chances are good that you'll have no plants native to your area. There may even be some exotic plants that have been shown to be invasive in the wildlands of Florida.

Removal of the invasive exotics needs to be started as soon as possible. You can probably remove invasive herbaceous plants, shrubs, and vines yourself or with some hired help. They don't have to be removed all at once, but the sooner you get rid of them, the sooner you can begin planting your natives. Removing invasive trees is a bigger job and you may need to call in an arborist to remove them, or if money is short, you could try to kill the trees by girdling them. Peel away a three-inch swath of bark all around near the base of the tree. This won't kill the tree right away, but eventually the top will not be able to receive the needed nutrients. Many trees will send up suckers in response, but if you keep removing the suckers, eventually the tree will die, leaving a snag in the landscape. Snags offer good ecosystem services in terms of shelter and food for the critters that will feast on the decaying wood. Girdling will not work on palms, but cutting off the tops will kill most of them; palm snags work well for habitat, too. It's best not to leave tall snags in areas where they could damage buildings, vehicles, or people when they fall, but maybe you can top them so they can still offer habitat with less risk of damaging something when they eventually fall.

On the other hand, well-behaved, noninvasive plants could remain in place permanently or temporarily while your new natives grow into their spots. You'll need a plan for handling the noninvasive exotics before you start planting an area with natives. For instance, you may have some overgrown Asian azaleas (*Rhododendron* spp.) that were used as foundation plants. Maybe you'd like to keep some of them, but in a new location where they can grow to their full size or become part of a hedgerow. Keep in mind that these exotic plants may not provide the same ecosystem services as natives, but these evergreen shrubs certainly can be useful in your landscape for screening and cover and they have already shown that they'll survive in your conditions. Successful transplanting of overgrown shrubs requires a lot of supplemental irrigation until the shrubs adapt to their new locations.

THE PLAN

Creating an overall plan is the fun part of this process, and working to the plan will save time and money in the long run. You should expect to modify the original plan as you learn about what works and what doesn't for you and your location. It is not realistic to expect that everything will prosper, but use the failures as lessons so you can try something else in those locations. This is why it's so important to keep good records of when you install your plants, where you bought them, and how well they did. Your log will be become an invaluable reference in years to come.

Plan for Tomorrow and for Today, Too

Once you decide to redo your landscape, it will be tempting to create an instant landscape, like you might see on TV. It's okay to install herbaceous plants in a dense

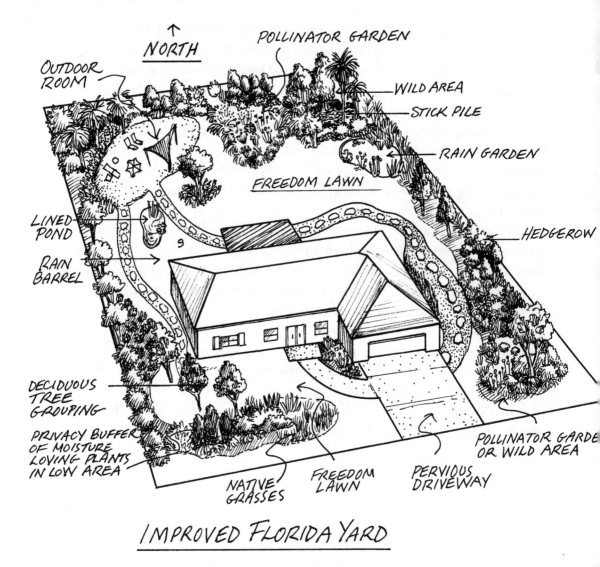

NORTH

OUTDOOR ROOM

POLLINATOR GARDEN

WILD AREA

STICK PILE

RAIN GARDEN

FREEDOM LAWN

HEDGEROW

LINED POND

RAIN BARREL

DECIDUOUS TREE GROUPING

PRIVACY BUFFER OF MOISTURE LOVING PLANTS IN LOW AREA

NATIVE GRASSES

FREEDOM LAWN

PERVIOUS DRIVEWAY

POLLINATOR GARDE OR WILD AREA

IMPROVED FLORIDA YARD

array for instant curb appeal and for habitat creation as soon as you remove chunks of your lawn. But don't plant your woody plants in dense patterns for curb appeal because it's very important to plan for the mature sizes of trees and shrubs; you'll need to plan for adequate distance both between the plants and from walkways or buildings. It's not smart to spend your valuable time hacking away at a shrub or tree that keeps getting in the way, so take the time to learn enough about woody plants before you purchase them so you know where they like to grow and how tall and how wide they'll become.

The Plan Needs to Include the Factor of Time

When your landscape is first planted, it may look sparse because it's best to use young, untopped trees and shrubs that will be quite small compared to their eventual sizes. As explained in Step 3, this is important because young plants will adapt much more quickly, and when they are planted together, groupings of young plants will mature together. The solution to this temporary sparse feeling is to fill the spaces between newly planted woody plants with herbaceous plants or container gardens. You could create a temporary butterfly garden or a meadow in your eventual tree grove. See Step 5 for details on butterfly gardens.

As the trees and shrubs grow, the nature of the space will change. When woody plants cast enough shade that the sun-loving meadow plants begin to suffer, it will be time to move the meadow plants to new, sunny locations. You could plant the areas near the trees with shade-tolerant ground covers and ferns, or you could let Mother Nature decide what should grow there with some guidance from you to keep the area clear of weedy plants. When the trees and shrubs shed enough of their own leaves and branches to create their own mulch, reduce the supplemental mulching. The ultimate goal of a grove in the landscape is to reach a state where you will just need to mulch the edges to maintain a neat mowing edge.

Living with Your Landscape

Many people implement their plans a little at a time as they have time, energy, and money. After gaining experience with natives in the landscape, feel free to alter your plan to take advantage of this hard-won knowledge. Guidelines are just that, but your experience with plants and plantings in your own landscape will provide information about unseen conditions in the soil that might influence the success or failure of the plantings.

Also, after living with the new landscape, you might change your mind about how big the outdoor room should be or decide that it might need more shade or more screening. You may find after a higher-than-average rainfall during a wet season that you need more rain barrels or that you need a larger capacity for stormwater storage in the area that absorbs the overflow from a pond.

Working in Sections

For both time and budget reasons, many people find that it works best to focus on one project at a time. This way they are not overwhelmed by a huge project. They can still implement the same overall plan, but one section at a time.

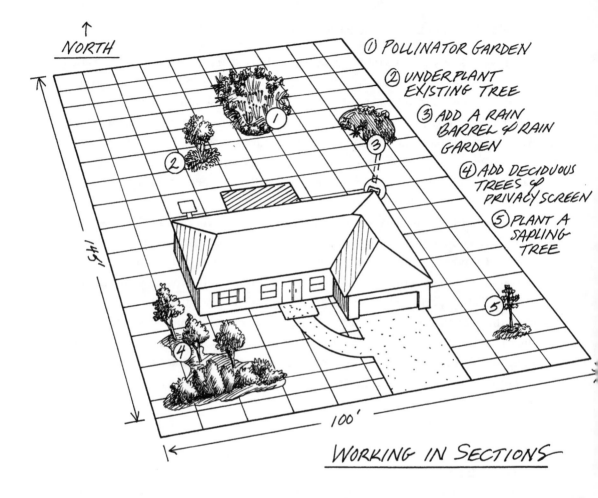

NORTH

① POLLINATOR GARDEN

② UNDERPLANT EXISTING TREE

③ ADD A RAIN BARREL & RAIN GARDEN

④ ADD DECIDUOUS TREES & PRIVACY SCREEN

⑤ PLANT A SAPLING TREE

145'

100'

WORKING IN SECTIONS

Make your own implementation plan that takes into account your budget, your time, and your neighborhood. Landscape changes may be better accepted if they are more gradual. For example, you might decide to tackle a couple of projects, like installing the privacy screening for the front yard, by putting understory plants under an existing tree, adding a drainage feature (a pair of rain barrels and a rain garden), or planting a simple pollinator garden.

Consult the next steps outlined in this book for ideas about how to be most successful with different types of plants and for various ways to implement the habitat modules. The approach you take to nativizing your yard and planning for a more sustainable landscape will depend on your situation. There is no one right way on the path to making these changes.

Whether you move quickly through the transformation process or slowly, everything you do will make a positive difference.

USE YOUR PLAN AS A GUIDELINE

While you should work hard to develop your master plan, reality may interfere with its implementation. A tree that you thought would be perfect might die or you may have to let everything sit as is for a long period if you are called away for a family emergency. When you are able to continue, your plan will still help guide your choices when you have an opportunity to begin the next step.

Having a plan will help when you're at a big native plant sale: you'll know what type of plants to look for and what roles the new plants are to play in your landscape. To be further prepared, bring a good Florida plant book for reference such as Gil Nelson's *Florida's Best Native Landscape Plants: 200 Readily Available Species for Homeowners and Professionals*, which includes information about size, companion plants, and growing conditions. Also bring your log with you so you can write down what you've bought—include pot sizes, prices, the name of the nursery, and details about the organization that organized the plant sale. Take notes on how big plants will get, other features of the plants, and how you'll be using them in your landscape. Take photos of the plants and their signs. If information sheets are offered, take those too.

STEP 2

Plan for Drainage and Stormwater Sequestration

Many Florida neighborhoods were constructed so that stormwater collected from roofs and other hard surfaces is piped directly out to impervious driveways and roads. Once on the road, the water will pick up pollutants that include drippage from vehicles, silt or sand, and trash before it goes into local stormwater system. Water that flows from landscapes, including lawns, will carry soil and organic substances from your yard and will pick up additional pollutants from driveways and roads. All of this ends up in the nearest waterway, where it damages the aquatic ecosystem with trash, too many nutrients, and toxic chemicals.

LANDSCAPES SHOULD ACT AS SPONGES

In order to improve water quality in nearby waterways, it's important that our landscapes soak up as much stormwater as possible. Some can be captured in rain barrels or a cistern, but the rest of the water will be absorbed by plants or will soak into the soil. The water that soaks into the soil will to add to the groundwater, and some of the groundwater may eventually reach and replenish our freshwater aquifers deep underground. We are sucking our aquifers dry with more and more demands for drinking water, but unfortunately much of our potable water is then used to irrigate unsustainable, greener-than-green lawns. One of the goals of this book is to reduce the demand for irrigation with sensible and sustainable landscaping ideas.

About 90 percent of the water that plants absorb is released as water vapor through the transpiration process. Some water will evaporate from the soil as well. The combined volume of the water transferred into the atmosphere from plants and from the soil is called the evapotranspiration rate. Air is cooled during the chemical process of water evaporation. This is the same thing that happens when you sweat; your body is cooled as the water evaporates.

You can increase the evapotranspiration rate for your landscape by increasing the leaf surface areas in your landscape. This means installing more plants and plants that will grow larger. When you do this, your landscape will not only absorb a greater volume of water, it will also be cooler.

There are four main benefits when our landscapes are designed to soak up more stormwater:

1) Nearby waterways will be less polluted.
2) The aquifers will possibly be refreshed with water that soaks into the soil.
3) The aquifers will have less pressure on them because of less use of irrigation due to use of collected stormwater and decreased lawn care.
4) The air around your home will be cooler as your plants mature.

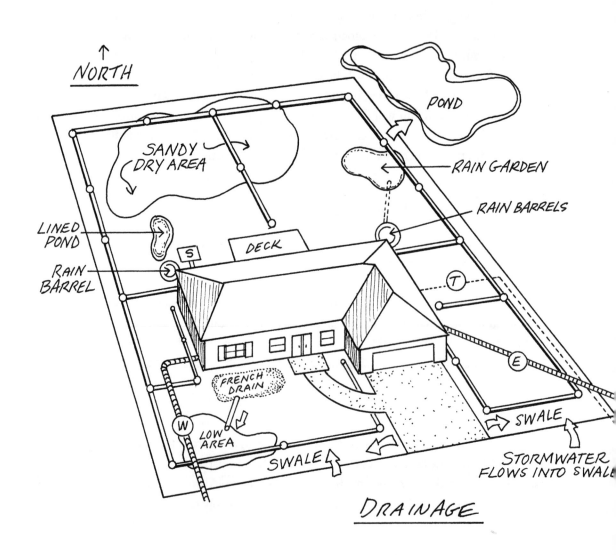

Planning for stormwater is tricky in Florida because we have a seven-month dry season and a five-month wet season from June through October, also known as hurricane season. This weather pattern is more dramatic in the peninsular region of the state and less dramatic in the Panhandle, but on average, Florida receives about twice as much rain during the wet season than it does during the seven-month dry season. The result is that there is often too much or not enough rain, but sometimes the wet season is drier than normal and sometimes there is significant rainfall during the dry season. Our plans need to be flexible and our plantings need to be able to withstand these fluctuations in moisture.

DESIGN THE LANDSCAPE TO ABSORB AND HANDLE MORE WATER

Before doing any major planting, arrange your landscape with features designed to soak up as much stormwater as possible. There are several methods for increasing water retention, including rain barrels, rain gardens, swales, dry wells, ponds, and other water features. Most well-designed landscapes will use a combination of these methods to handle water for differing landscape situations.

As discussed in Step 1, the property assessment should include what happens during and after a heavy rain. There may be low places that stay wet after a rain where moisture-loving plants such as mosses, rushes, and ferns may already be growing. Some landscape wet spots will hold water for days. If your property abuts a roadside swale, this would be a wet area as well. It's also important to know the really dry spots in your landscape so you can use only drought-tolerant plants there.

WATER IS A PRECIOUS RESOURCE: DON'T FLUSH IT AWAY

It's important for the health of Florida's waterways to capture as much stormwater as possible on your property. This is particularly important if your property backs up to or is near a body of water, including stormwater retention ponds.

As part of your goal to soak up as much stormwater as possible, you may wish to replace impervious pavement in your landscape with interlocking pavers, gravel topped with stepping stones, wooden decking, or other surface materials that allow water to soak in. Consider this change in drainage when designing the rest of your landscape. A chronically wet spot on the low side of a solid cement driveway could become much drier after you replace the cement with a pervious surface.

If you break up a cement surface, the pieces could be useful as stepping-stones, retention walls, or gravel in dry wells. Repurposing used cement, also known as urbanite, is certainly more sustainable than discarding it. Some people work on replacing cement a little at a time as they have time and energy. This process could be started where cracks develop due to sinking or uplifting where tree roots are pushing it up. Trees are stronger than cement and if happens on your property, you may wish to alter the driveway path to accommodate the roots.

If you plan to add soil to build a berm in your landscape as part of a screening project, make sure that it won't create new drainage problems. (See Step 4 for more on screening.) For instance, stormwater could collect between the new high spot and your house that might make a muddy mess after a heavy rain just outside your doorways, along your paths, or next to your deck or patio. Even worse, the collected moisture could possibly leak into your house or undermine its foundation. Compensate for trapped stormwater with a catch basin, a rain garden, and/ or a French drain to take the excess water to a safe spot in your landscape where water can soak in.

If you'll be making significant changes in elevation one way or another around your house and other buildings, this will alter the flow of stormwater. It might be best to hire a civil engineer or landscape architect to save you from big and potentially expensive problems. The other goal of a professionally designed drainage system is to ensure that stormwater sequestration is adequate. This will contribute to healthier waterways.

PLAN FOR REDUCED USE OF YOUR IRRIGATION SYSTEM

If there is an automated irrigation system in place, plan to reduce its use as you decrease the size of your lawn and change to more sustainable and less-irrigated lawn care for what's left. As your mostly native yard matures, it will require less and less supplemental irrigation. If irrigation had been used frequently enough to keep a lawn green on a year-round basis, then there may be artificially created wet areas that may dry up as you move away from frequent watering.

Some people completely remove their irrigation systems as part of moving to a more native landscape, but keeping an existing system in place may be a good idea to help newly installed plants become established and in the long run to keep your plants in good shape during extended droughts. If you decide to keep the system, make sure it has a rain sensor that turns it off if there has been significant rain. Better yet, switch to a manual system that you turn it on only when necessary. Existing sprinkler heads may need to be relocated or elevated—ones that are at ground level (mowable) would be replaced with ones that sit on elevated pipes that would work well in places where the vegetation is taller. You may also need to reduce the number of sprinkler heads in some places to fit in better with your new landscaping.

Another option is to replace spray irrigation systems with more water-efficient drip systems, either temporarily during the establishment phase of their new native plantings or permanently. When water is sprayed in the air, much of it evaporates and some of it hits hard surfaces due to wind, poorly designed coverage, or inadequate maintenance of sprayer heads. With drip irrigation, micro emitters direct water only to areas where it is needed. Installing drip irrigation systems is relatively simple and can be accomplished without professional help. Supplies are readily available at hardware stores. Do your research on installing drip irrigation systems and plan for the filtration and pressure regulation that will be needed to make the switch from a high-pressure system.

SEQUESTERING STORMWATER

Florida receives an average of fifty to sixty inches of rain annually, but because of our wet and dry seasons, often there is too much water or too little. Several inches of rain could fall in one day during tropical storms, so plan your landscape to handle this. On the other hand, some months will have virtually no rain during the dry season, so your plants will need to handle this as well.

GUIDING STORMWATER THROUGH YOUR LANDSCAPE

To make the best use of natural precipitation, you can sequester it in several ways, even on a small lot, but your water-sequestering features may not be right next to each other. So before you install features for sequestering water, plan to guide the water from one feature to the next, creating a stormwater flow chain. For instance, water from a downspout could flow into a series of two rain barrels. The overflow from the second one could go into a blind drain that goes under a path and drains into a small, lined pond that overflows into a rain garden. The overflow from the rain garden could flow into a wooded area that can absorb the excess water safely away from the house or other buildings.

A blind drain or French drain is usually invisible or nearly so in the landscape. It gathers water from one location and guides it through a pipe to another location. Begin your French drain with a dry well of coarse gravel encased in landscape fabric. Abut a four- or six-inch drainpipe against the side of the dry well near the

STORMWATER FLOW CHAIN

surface of the soil. (The open end of the drainpipe should be covered with cloth to keep out soil and critters but porous enough to allow good water flow—used panty hose legs work well.) Bury the pipe with a downward slope under the path to the top of the pond. The exit end of the pipe should also be covered with cloth. In another situation, you could use a length of perforated drain pipe covered with a cloth sock (these socks are sold with this type of pipe) to absorb water along a gutterless eave or along an impervious driveway.

While much of Florida is flat, some landscapes may have enough of a slope that stormwater rushes downward, carrying soil, leaves, and mulch. To interrupt this flow, build a curved barrier across the slope. It usually works best to build the barrier with a combination of plants and soil or soil-like materials. The curve of the barrier will catch the water, but you'll need a plan to handle this collected water. You could build a rain garden or a dry well right there or you could install a blind drain to move the water to another location—maybe all three.

It's a good idea to use biologs to build berms in the landscape, because they reduce possible erosion. A biolog is a biodegradable tube of fabric that is filled with compost, straw, sawdust, wood chips, or other organic materials. Normally, it is filled on site and then stapled in place with wooden stakes. In some projects, the stakes could be freshly cut from easily rootable trees or shrubs, such as willows or wax myrtles.

WATER SEQUESTRATION FEATURES

Rain Barrels

Install rain barrels at some of the downspouts on your house or other buildings. A closed rain barrel system overflows back into the drainage system in place when it's full, while an open rain barrel system diverts all of the downspout water to a barrel or series of barrels and overflows out into the landscape or into a designed drainage system of French drains, rain gardens, ponds, and/or dry wells.

Knowing how much water to expect will inform decisions you make about water sequestration features. Calculate the surface area of the roof as if it were flat by pacing off the walls. Multiply the length times the width and then multiply by 0.6 and by the inches of rainfall. For instance, one half-inch of rain on 1,000 square feet of roof will generate 300 gallons of water.

$$(L \times W \text{ [in feet]}) \times 0.6 \times \text{inches of rain} = \text{gallons of water}$$

Typical rain barrels have a 55-gallon capacity. Having more than one at each downspout will increase the capacity. This way you can save more water for use during those long dry periods. Some people like the idea of a large-capacity cistern to store even more water. A cistern can be buried; this might make the most sense for a small landscape. If you have a cistern, pipe all of your downspout outflows to it through underground French drains. Whether the water you store in cisterns is above or below ground, to use it, you will probably need to install a small pump to provide adequate pressure.

Water from rain barrels and cisterns is free from synthetic chemicals, so it won't kill the microbes that are so important in compost and in healthy soils. In addition to using it to water plants, you can use it for wetting compost piles, pre-rinsing vegetables, rinsing tools, pre-rinsing dirty garden clothing, in temporary drip irrigation systems set up for newly planted trees and shrubs until they become established, and more. Making good use of your rain barrel water for your gardening needs will save on the use of potable water, which is becoming more and more precious these days.

Rain barrel water provides savings for a sunny day.

Rain Gardens

It's a good idea to build at least one rain garden in a natural or manufactured swale to receive stormwater from downspouts or rain barrels or runoff from a driveway or other hardscape features. Plant it with a selection of plants that can withstand standing water and can also tolerate drought during Florida's seven-month dry season. Because of our dry season, the list of rain garden plants for Florida differs from

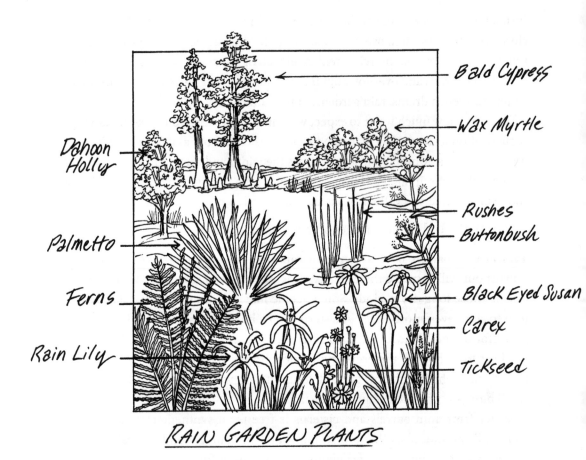

RAIN GARDEN PLANTS

lists for other regions even if the plants are native to Florida. For instance, cardinal flower, which is native to Florida, is a recommended rain garden plant for the Mid-Atlantic region, but it needs to be damp or wet all the time. It would need to be watered to survive our dry seasons in a rain garden, and that defeats the whole goal of a sustainable rain garden.

Herbaceous plants for that are recommended for Florida rain gardens include black-eyed Susan, mistflower, blue-eyed grass, Dixie iris, goldenrod, meadow beauty, rain lily, most ferns, meadow garlic, rushes, sedges, and some grasses. Woody plants recommended for Florida rain gardens include bald and pond cypress, buttonbush, cabbage palm, dahoon holly, dwarf and saw palmettos, elderberry, inkberry, wax myrtle, sweetbay magnolia, and red maple.

Once stormwater flows into the rain garden, it can soak into the ground or be absorbed by the plants in or around the rain garden. Larger plants with abundant leaf surface area absorb more water than smaller plants because the transpiration volume depends on the number of stomata (pores) in the leaves where water can evaporate into the air.

The sandier the soil, the faster the water will be absorbed. If your soil is clayey or rocky, you could build a big dry well in the middle of the rain garden to increase its capacity without making the garden itself too much deeper than the surrounding landscape. You can also make it larger, depending on your landscape situation, to absorb more water. The goal of a well-designed rain garden is for it to be empty within about three days of a rain event to prevent mosquitoes from breeding there.

Plan for the rain garden overflow, too, because in Florida tropical storms can drop several inches of rain a day. Make sure it will overflow away from buildings, paths, and other infrastructure. The overflow could be handled with a small dry well that feeds a French drain that takes it to a bigger dry well or to a wild area. The rain garden will be a feature in your landscape, but the drainage will be invisible, so make sure that it can withstand the pressures for that section of your landscape. If cars or other vehicles will be rolling over your drainpipe, provide good support for it or have it deep enough that the weight will not crush it.

Rain gardens can be designed with only herbaceous plants to preserve a view or maintain visibility. These rain gardens can also serve as butterfly gardens or wilder meadow areas in your landscape. You may also use rain gardens in tandem with a pond, usually as an outflow area, but it could also be an inflow area so the stormwater has a chance to settle in before heading into the pond. It depends on the situation.

Ponds

Adding ponds and other water features to your landscape helps create good habitat. Ponds also serve as interesting focal points and as places to use moisture-loving plants. In a small landscape, it's likely that your pond will be built using a pre-formed liner or a plastic sheet to line a hole that you dig. These small ponds are great, but they don't help very much with the water absorption in your landscape because they are lined. The areas around lined ponds may be able to sustain moisture-loving plants because the liner keeps the area artificially wet.

On the other hand, you could incorporate a lined pond within the stormwater flow chain in your landscape. For instance, you could direct the outflow from one downspout that has one or more rain barrels into the pond, which would then drain into a rain garden, a dry well, or a wild area that can absorb the leftover water. This way your pond water would change frequently and this might reduce the need to clean out algae and other muck that tends to gather in artificial ponds.

An unlined stormwater pond could accept some or all of the stormwater. This type of pond also offers important habitat values that support natural predators in

WETLAND CREATURES

your local ecosystem. A stormwater pond would probably be seasonal: it will fill up during the wet season but may be empty during most of the dry season but still muddy enough to offer shelter to the pond critters. To plan for deluges, build it as large as is practical for your landscape, but it will still need an overflow area that directs excess water away from buildings.

A seasonal pond is similar to a rain garden and should be planted with mostly rain garden plants, especially around the edges and in the shallows. It's a good idea to stock either type of pond with native mosquitofish.

Dry Wells

To add more storage capacity for stormwater, dig at least one high-capacity dry well that can accept the overflows from ponds, rain barrels, and/or rain gardens. Dry wells are especially useful if your soil does not drain well naturally. These are invisible in the landscape but can play an important part in increasing your stormwater capacity, especially on small lots or in high-use areas. A dry well can be placed in a chronically wet area to soak up the moisture or it can be placed in a better draining area where French drains have been installed to transport water from downspouts or other stormwater collection areas. Be sure to angle the pipes of French drains for good drainage to the dry well.

The size of a dry well will be determined by the porosity of the soil and by the volume of water that will be directed into it. Before deciding on the location of a dry well, dig a test hole that is one foot square and as deep as you estimate you will need during the wet season. Let it sit for half a day and look for seepage into the hole. If water seeps in, don't put your dry well there—dig a pond there instead. If no water seeps in, fill the hole with water to see how long it takes to drain out. The longer it takes to drain, the larger your dry-well hole needs to be. These drainage tests should be done during the wet season and not too long after a good rain.

Dry wells work on the principle that you will replace the soil with something with larger gaps that accepts a higher volume of water. The water can then sit there until it soaks into the ground without altering the human use of that area. A simple dry well consists of a hole filled with coarse gravel covered with a bed of mulch or even a lawn so that its presence in the landscape is not obvious. To make it work more efficiently, line the hole on all sides (including the top) with geotextile fabric (weed barrier cloth) to keep out the soil. To increase the storage for water, include some porous containers buried with the gravel. These could be donuts of cloth-covered porous drainage pipes or covered, porous buckets or other containers that are strong enough to support the weight of the gravel on top of them plus the weight of people or machinery that may run over the top of them.

Vignette: A Tale of Two Jamaica Capers (*Quadrella jamaicensis*)

A South Florida homeowner bought two of these great native shrubs at a plant sale. She planted one about five feet away from the edge of the roadside swale at the front of her property and the other one in a much drier section of the property. Both sites were partly sunny and seemed to be more or less the same except for the proximity to the swale.

The homeowner knew that the caper is a drought-tolerant plant, but she did not think that the proximity to the swale would make much of a difference. After three years, the shrub in the dry spot was more than six feet tall and very bushy, while the one near the swale had not grown much beyond its original eighteen inches. It didn't look terrible, but when compared to its companion, it had been clearly stunted by the wet habitat.

It's very important to match the moisture levels in your landscape and to the moisture preferences of the plants you choose. If a plant needs more moisture (especially during its initial adjustment period), you can irrigate, but if a plant is not tolerant of wet soil, there is no easy way to make it less moist.

Water can be directed to the dry well through French drains from overflow areas of ponds, rain barrels, or rain gardens. The end of the French drain can intersect with the dry well below its top to accommodate enough of an angle for drainage.

You would normally plant herbaceous or ground cover plants over the top of a dry well, but nearby water-loving trees such as red maples or willows will seek out the water and help drain the area.

Roadside Swales

Many communities are built with roadside swales that receive and handle stormwater from roads and parking lots. If you have one of these community-owned swales bordering your property, learn what is allowed and whether you are expected to maintain it. Sometimes the county will not tolerate anything that is not turf grass and they may mow it once or twice a year to maintain roadside visibility.

If you're lucky, you may be able to treat this like a rain garden and plant the road

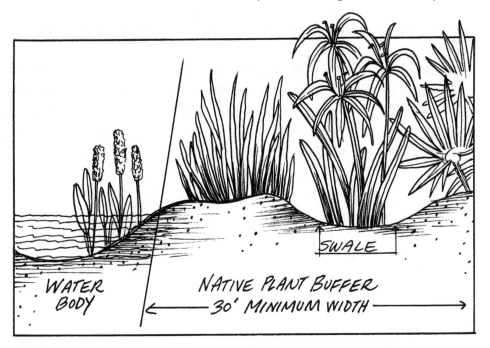

USE BUFFER ZONES TO LIMIT RUNOFF

side of the swale with herbaceous plants like rushes and black-eyed Susans to keep good visibility. On your side of the swale, you may be able to plant moisture-loving trees and shrubs for privacy and greater water absorption.

AT THE WATER'S EDGE

If a property borders the edge of a wetland or a body of water, it's best to create a buffer area of thick plantings to intercept or slow the flow of water from your property, especially if there is a slope. This buffer may also protect your property from erosion due to waves or storm surges coming from the water. To be the most effective, the buffer should be twenty or thirty feet wide, but any buffer planting is better than none. In some communities, there are rules about what can and cannot be planted along the water's edge.

It's a good idea to create a berm or swale parallel to the shoreline in your buffer to form a sort of long rain garden where the water can soak in. If you'd like to maintain your view of the water, use low-growing herbaceous plants such as bunching grasses mixed with wildflowers. If the area is damp or subject to occasional flooding, use plants recommended for rain gardens. If the water is salty, adjust your plant list accordingly.

If there is a path to the water's edge, build it so it winds its way to the water instead of heading straight down. Use stepping-stones, pavers, or raised decking to reduce soil erosion and to improve footing. Both of these actions will also slow the water flow from your property to the shoreline.

STEP 3

Install Trees

Woody plants, trees and shrubs, are sometimes referred to as the bones of a landscape. They are the largest and will have a large impact on how a landscape looks and feels. The dividing line between what is a tree and what is a shrub can get hazy (shrubs are addressed in Step 4). Furthermore, some plants that serve as trees and shrubs in the landscape may not actually produce any real wood, such as palm trees and coonties.

While many people, especially commercial landscapers, plant all the trees and shrubs all at once, it may be a good idea to plant the trees first and then plant the understory plants a year or two later. This way the trees will be well established and will have begun to cast some shade, so their understory plants, which are chosen because of their ability to thrive in the partial shade under trees, will have the environment they prefer.

CHOOSING WHICH TREES TO PLANT

Select tree species that will not outgrow their allotted spaces in the landscape, in both width and height. Planning for the mature tree size is especially important for small properties. This way you'll avoid the need for ongoing excessive pruning and trimming or, worse, taking out a misplaced tree. Do the preliminary research before going to a local native nursery or a native plant sale. For starters, generate a likely plant list by type for your county using the Florida Native Plant Society website (www.fnps. org/plants).

There are a number of good books and online resources on Florida's native plants (see the list at the end of the introduction), but one of the most useful resources for developing a landscape is Gil Nelson's *Florida's Best Native Landscape Plants: 200 Readily Available Species for Homeowners and Professionals*. It provides details

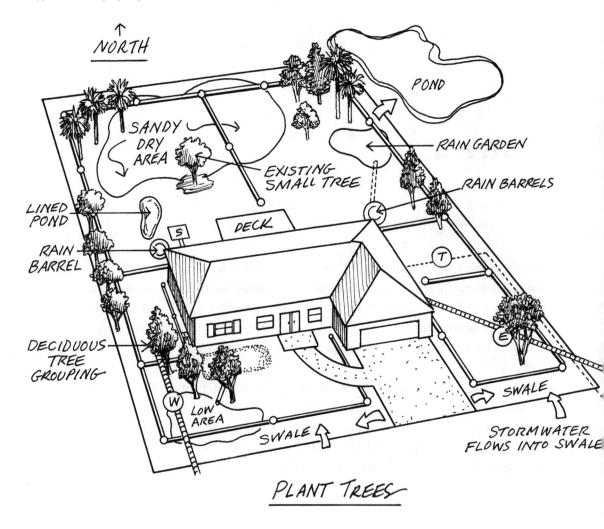

NORTH

POND

SANDY
DRY
AREA

RAIN GARDEN

EXISTING
SMALL TREE

RAIN BARRELS

LINED
POND

DECK

S

T

RAIN
BARREL

DECIDUOUS
TREE
GROUPING

E

W

LOW
AREA

SWALE

SWALE

STORMWATER
FLOWS INTO SWALE

PLANT TREES

about size, where to plant, soil requirements, and what to plant with each of the 200 plants. Nelson wrote it with the help of the Florida Association of Native Nurseries, so these plants are likely to be available in the native nursery trade.

The next step is to take your tree and shrub list when you visit parks or botanical gardens that feature native landscapes and identify the plants with labels. Or go on field trips to areas near where you live with your local FNPS chapter. This way you can see how your selected trees work in a natural setting. Then visit a nursery that sells natives or go to a native plant sale and talk to the vendors to see what they have to say about your list. This may seem like a lot of work, but trees are a long-term investment and your research will increase the chances that they will succeed in the landscape.

Dioecious Species

Individual plants that are dioecious will bear either male and female flowers but usually not both. In other words, an individual plant will be male or female. If you choose a dioecious species to add to your landscape and you want fruit to form, make sure that there is at least one male plant in your neighborhood.

Quite a few Florida natives fall into this category. Examples include maples (*Acer* spp.), hollies (*Ilex* spp.), willows (*Salix* spp.), red cedar (*Juniperus virginiana*), wax myrtle (*Morella cerifera*), and coontie (*Zamia integrifolia*). Some of these, like hollies, junipers, and wax myrtles, you would want to have fruit for showiness and to feed the birds. Others, like maples, not so much.

If you decide to use a dioecious species and you want fruit, ask the vendor what the gender of the plant is, but if it's grown from seed, it's likely that you won't know what you have until it produces flowers. Plants that are grown from cuttings are clones of plants and the gender will be known. For instance, the dwarf yaupon holly (*Ilex vomitoria* 'Nana') is a known male and will never have berries, but if you have it in your landscape, female holly plants will be fertilized even if they are a different species.

SELECTING THE BEST SPECIMENS

While it's tempting to purchase larger tree specimens to make more of an impact in your new landscaping right away, it's rarely worth the extra money, the extra water, or the extra work needed to acclimate them to the landscape. A younger tree will adjust much more readily and will usually catch up to the larger tree specimen within only a few years. In addition, a tree planted when it is young is much more likely to live out its full life cycle. They are a long-term investment. (See the sidebar.)

You want your trees to be:

Young

Purchase only young trees that are less than one-inch caliper. (Caliper for saplings is the diameter of the trunk at six inches above the root flare.) These young trees will not have been held in containers for too long, so the roots should be in pretty good shape. (The exception is field-grown trees that are extracted and planted by large machines. They have a fairly high rate of success and will have an instant impact in your landscape. This includes our native cabbage palm trees, which are almost always sold as mature specimens dug from the field. This option is quite expensive compared to the cost of hand-planted specimens.)

Untopped

Tree specimens that have not been cut off are often called whips. In the long run, these trees will be much stronger than trees that have been trimmed to make them bushy. Growers sometimes trim trees to cater to the old (but incorrect) advice that we should buy the bushiest plants. That may be okay advice for shrubs, but not for trees. Here are some reasons not to buy topped trees:

- A single trunk is the strongest, most wind-resistant form for a tree. This is important for Florida landscapes because of the number of tropical storms that could occur over the tree's life cycle.
- It will take years of corrective pruning to create a new leader from the branches that sprout after a top is chopped.
- A topped tree will often have a shorter life because the spot where it was topped will be a weak spot into the future.

Dormant (If Possible)

Depending on whether the tree is deciduous or not and your location in the state, it may be a good idea to purchase trees that have lost their leaves for the season. This way, the trees do not have the stress of keeping leaves turgid while their roots are adjusting. In frost-free zones in South Florida, this is less of a possibility, so if this is where you live, you may want to time the tree planting with the beginning of the wet season in the summer to reduce the need for additional irrigation.

Buying small trees saves time and money.

ARRANGING TREES IN THE LANDSCAPE

Plan to have trees and shrubs where they will deliver the most benefits in your landscape, whether it's shading or screening. If there is enough space in the landscape, group an odd number of trees in a grove. As you plant, plan for their mature sizes so they'll have adequate room to grow, but plant them close enough so they will form a continuous canopy as they mature. If the landscape is too small for a grouping of trees, create a grove by planting a single tree surrounded by tall and medium-sized shrubs with a low layer of herbaceous plants intermingled with and outside the shrub layer.

The Case for Not Buying Large Container-Grown Trees

The definition of large tree for this discussion is one with more than a two-inch caliper. While it's tempting to purchase larger tree specimens to make the most impact in your new landscaping, don't do it.

STUNTED ROOTS

A tree that has been confined to a container for the years necessary to grow to a good size will be plagued with circling and stunted roots. This makes it much less likely to survive, no matter how well it is cared for during and after planting.

BURIED ROOT FLARE

Quite often when a tree is moved to larger pots as it grows it will be planted deep enough to keep it upright, which buries the root flare in the soil. For various reasons, trees do much better over the long run when the root flare is above the soil line. Some species may form adventitious roots above the root flare, which will make it difficult to find the original root flare. Note: Only trees grown from seed will have root flares. Trees grown from cuttings will not have them.

DIFFICULTY ADJUSTING TO A DIFFERENT SOIL

Container-grown trees will be adapted to a rich growing medium and lots of fertilizer. Larger trees will have difficulty adjusting to the regular soil in your landscape.

WEAKNESS FROM BEING TOPPED

Larger trees are likely to have been topped so they would fit into a van for transport. As discussed elsewhere, topped trees have a shortened life and will not be as strong as an uncut tree.

LOWER LIKELIHOOD OF SURVIVAL

Because of all these reasons, a larger, container-grown tree is much less likely to thrive and much more likely to die. It's rarely worth the money and the additional effort needed to acclimate them to your landscape. A younger tree will adjust much more quickly and will usually catch up to the larger tree specimen within only a few years and with a lot less work and a lot less water.

PLANT TREES IN GROUPS

A grouping of trees and shrubs has a number of benefits over single specimen trees:

- They are more wind tolerant.
- Both the trees and the shrubs will have more drought tolerance because they will create their own beneficial microclimate when they are grown together.
- They will offer good habitat for birds and other wildlife, especially if there is some vegetation cover from the ground into the canopy.
- This planting scheme cools the landscape because of the dense biomass and the large volume of transpiration.
- Less and less maintenance will be needed for the interior spaces in a grove as the woody plants mature. There may be occasional, bird-planted invasive plants that will have to be removed, but the area will eventually

become self-mulching and because the soil will be disturbed less and less, fewer weeds will sprout. Eventually only the edges will need occasional maintenance.

CHOOSING TREES TO GROUP TOGETHER

For a small lot or a small space on a larger lot, where there is room for three trees, it's probably best to choose just one tree species. Choose specimens with different heights and branching patterns. This variation will make your grouping look more natural. If there is room for five or more trees, you could select more than one species, but make sure they are compatible in terms of soil preferences and moisture levels. This is where your research trips to parks and other natural areas can help you create realistic and viable combinations. If you've seen two or more tree species growing together in a natural area in a local park or other wild space, use that as a guideline for how to group them in your landscape.

PLANT FOR THE FUTURE

After you purchase trees, set them out in the landscape at their planned spots while they are still in their pots. Look at them from all angles, including from inside the house and from decks or patios. Look at views that are open and those that may be blocked once the trees grow. Some people find it helpful to mark where the eventual canopy will be with lime, paint, string, or hoses. Depending on your situation, you may want to see how it looks from across the street and as you walk by. You could also take photos of the landscape with the potted trees in place from all these angles as well. Then take a photo and draw the outline of mature-sized trees in the photo. This may help you better visualize the adult tree sizes and the roles they will eventually play in your landscape.

Don't hurry the visualization stage, because this is when your plan will begin to come to life—when you will begin to imagine how your landscape will "feel." You may want to invite other members of your household and/or fellow gardeners into your landscape so you can walk and talk them through your plan. This will give you feedback. In addition, as you explain what you are trying to accomplish, you may come up with some new ideas. When you consider eventual sizes on location, you may need to rearrange your planting scheme, but this is okay. It's much better to change your plans now, before you plant any trees, than to realize a few years down the road that you needed more space for a path or that a favorite view will be blocked.

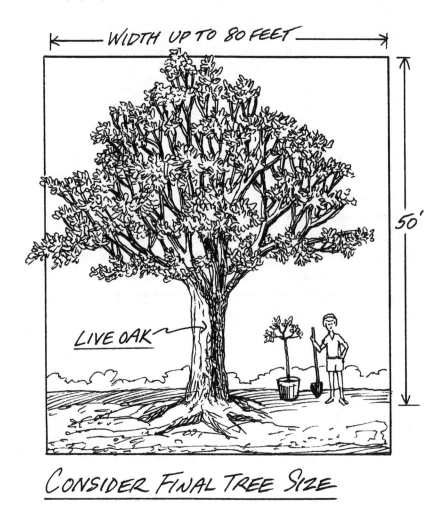

WIDTH UP TO 80 FEET

50'

LIVE OAK

CONSIDER FINAL TREE SIZE

THE PLANTING

The best way to plant a container-grown tree is to soak the container the day before you plant. On planting day, clear each planting space of lawn or weeds and dig a wide shallow hole for each of the trees. Rinse all the soil away from the roots and untangle the root mass. Use a bucket or a small tub to simplify the process. You may add the slurry of the potting soil and water to your compost pile, but don't put it in the planting hole. (University studies are still under way on bare-rooting and tree survival, but Linda Chalker-Scott's "Horticultural Techniques for Successful Plant Establishment" [http://drought.wsu.edu/wp-content/uploads/sites/5/2015/06/Horticultural-Techniques-for-successful-plant-establishment.pdf] provides good information. Chalker-Scott is a professor of horticulture at Washington State University.)

Bring the bare-rooted tree to the hole and spread the roots in all directions in the shallow hole. Make sure that the root flare is at least a couple of inches above the soil level and that the center of the planting hole has a solid central mound so the main tree trunk will not sink. You may need to dig the hole wider or deeper to accommodate all the roots. Hopefully there will not be any circling roots that are so woody that they cannot be straightened out, but if there are, urge them outward without breaking them if possible. However, if they are too woody, cut them cleanly so the circle is broken.

Add soil you have dug up from the hole and then add water to the hole to mud in the roots. Do not add anything else—no fertilizer, no compost, nothing. Keep adding mud to the stretched-out roots (but not on top of the root flare) and pat down until the tree is stable. In some cases, you may need to add a temporary stake with soft cloth ties to keep the tree upright, but remove the ties as soon as possible so the tree learns to support itself.

Build a circular two-inch high berm of soil around the tree just inside the outer-most roots. Make this berm taller if the tree is planted on a slope because water will tend to drain away more readily. This will help keep water in the root ball area during

RINSE AWAY SOIL AND STRAIGHTEN CIRCLING ROOTS

the adjustment phase. After this process, water again. The rule of thumb is to use one three-gallon watering can to mud in the roots and another one for irrigation after planting. Add a two-inch layer of mulch such as wood chips both inside and outside the berm, but not right against the tree trunk. Mulch helps keep down the weeds, helps hold the moisture, and helps moderate fluctuations in soil temperature.

Unless there is a soaking rain of half an inch or more, you will need to irrigate the newly planted tree over and above landscape-wide irrigation. The amount and extent of the irrigation depends on the soil type and the size of the tree. The rule of thumb is for a tree that's less than two-inch caliper, irrigate with three gallons of water per caliper inch daily for two weeks, then every other day for two months, then weekly until the tree is established, which could be three to eight months. (See Edward F. Gilman, "Irrigating Landscape Plants during Establishment," http://edis. ifas.ufl.edu/ep113.)

After a few weeks, you can add a compost top dressing outside the berm. Don't dig it in, but do add mulch on top of it. The compost will condition the soil outside the planting hole with some nutrients but mostly with its microbes so the roots will grow out. A few months later you can add another ring of compost, but this ring should be even farther from the tree. This compost should be made from local plant materials only—do not add any manures or other super-fertile materials. You don't want to push the tree into unsustainable growth; all you want to do is encourage the roots to grow outward. You may repeat the compost top dressing a few more times over the first couple of years. Each circle should be farther away from the tree than the previous one.

As you urge the roots outward, the tree will become more drought tolerant and more wind tolerant. These are important attributes for its long-term survival in Florida, so this minimum amount of work is an investment for the future.

WHILE YOU WAIT

Plant small tree specimens ten or more feet apart, depending on their mature size specifications. The landscape may look sparsely planted, but you are not planting for curb appeal today; you are planting for the future. While waiting for the trees to gain some height, either leave existing plants in place or plant sun-loving natives such as butterfly plants, meadow wildflowers, or bunching grasses to fill in the spaces between them. Container gardens or trellises could also fill in the spaces.

If the young trees are surrounded with meadow plants, be sure to mark them well with stakes, ribbons, or even wire cages so they don't get mowed down. This is especially important if someone else is working on landscape maintenance. Also, if there are deer or other large herbivores in the vicinity, protect your young trees with a combination of wire fencing and netting.

The ideal time to plant the shrubs and other understory plants called for in your plan is when your new trees have grown enough to produce some shade. Don't rush this stage because the plants you have selected for planting in groupings near trees will usually do best with some shade. The plants you have selected to be nearest the trees, such as ferns, will require a deeper shade, so plant them last. Shrubs and other plants that will be located at or around the eventual drip lines

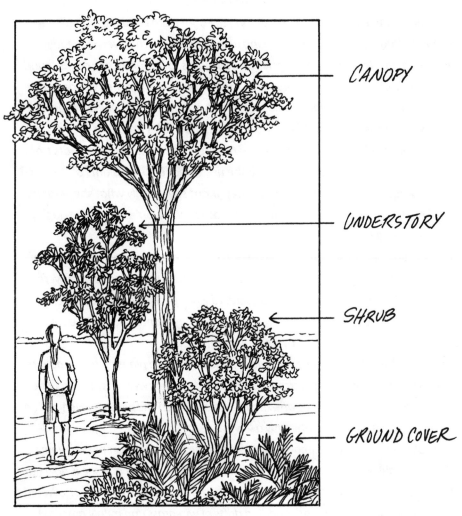

CANOPY

UNDERSTORY

SHRUB

GROUND COVER

VEGETATION LEVELS

Vignette: The Slow and Steady Road to a Native Yard

At the outset, an east coast Florida yard was mostly lawn and exotic plants, some of which were invasive, like the large chinaberry tree that loomed over the house in a side yard. The owner's goals included creating shade on the south side of the house to cut energy use and planting thick privacy screening that would limit the view of her home from neighboring yards, especially a two-story home that faced directly onto her backyard patio area.

The owner wanted to economize by doing much of the work on her own but was initially limited by the difficulty of getting the right plants and the high cost of removing large exotics. Instead of giving up and planting whatever was readily available, she started slowly, adding her desired plants to the landscape as she found them. From start to finish, installation took roughly ten years, but the extended time-table provided the owner with an enjoyable and manageable gardening project.

Plants were mostly sourced from local native plant sales and from friends' yards, although a few specimen plants were purchased in three-gallon pots from regional native plant nurseries. Because she used smaller-sized plants at the outset, the homeowner was able to save money, plant specifically what she wanted, and take advantage of volunteer plants that otherwise would have been dug up and thrown away.

The homeowner chose plant species in response to site needs such as the size of the available planting area, easements, and soil types. Large, invasive trees were girdled and de-limbed until only snags useful to woodpeckers and insects were left. By the time the invasive trees were gone, the newly planted native tree canopy was mature enough to function as a shady hammock.

Several native cabbage palms in the yard added height, so planting small sapling trees was possible. Small trees were more practical since they were easy to carry and fit in the owner's car. She learned an expensive lesson when she planted seven-gallon slash pines that began to die after only a few years. After that, she only used smaller-sized plants since they acclimated better to the site than the larger potted plants.

The owner did not make a plan at the beginning of the project and she is now updating sections of her yard to give it a more landscaped look. She has also discovered the beauty of native grasses and is adding drifts of wiregrass and muhly grass to her yard. She is still enjoying tinkering with the right combination of plants.

should be more tolerant of a mostly sunny location, so it's fine to plant them only one or two years after the trees have been planted.

However, some people have success when they plant the trees and shrubs all at once to make a more immediate impact in the landscape. At first the shrubs may grow more quickly than the trees, which may urge the trees to grow faster to seek more sunlight. When all the woody plants are grown together like this, their roots mingle naturally. If you install all the woody plants together, make sure that the shrubs are adaptable enough to withstand the full sun for those first few years while the trees are gaining height and also make sure that they will also tolerate the partial shade once the trees grow taller.

WHEN YOU PLANT A TREE YOU BELIEVE IN THE FUTURE

We are lucky in Florida because our rainfall is more than adequate to support trees in our landscapes. Trees are long-term investments and it's important to visualize how they will look in your landscape many years down the road. Maybe one day your grandchildren's children will be sitting on a swing hung from a branch of a tree that you planted.

STEP 4

Plant Shrubs

The dividing line between what is a tree and what is a shrub is not particularly clear, but an often-used rule of thumb is that a shrub grows to less than fifteen feet tall and usually has multiple stems or canes, while a tree is taller than fifteen feet and has a single trunk. (You can probably think of exceptions off the top of your head.) Furthermore, a small tree could serve as a shrub in your landscape, or a tall shrub could serve as a tree, especially in a small landscape.

You should follow the guidelines for trees when choosing shrubs, both the species and the specific specimens, but here are some general exceptions for shrubs:

- Don't worry about whether they have been trimmed back. A bushier bush is fine if it suits your needs in the landscape.
- Newly planted shrubs usually adapt more quickly than trees, so you can probably purchase ones that are a little more mature to make a greater impact in your landscape. But buying younger specimens will still save water, time, and money.
- Pay close attention to the projected size, especially the width and tendency to sucker, especially in small landscapes. A dwarf yaupon holly cultivar is slow growing and will probably be small and cute when you buy it, but in a few years it could grow to seven feet tall and ten feet wide and will send up suckers quite a distance from the original bush. This would be okay for a wild area or a thick hedgerow, but it's not a particularly good plant for a tight location, despite the word "dwarf" in its name.

THERE ARE MANY WAYS TO USE SHRUBS IN YOUR LANDSCAPE

Shrubs can have many uses in the landscape, but in traditional landscapes shrubs have often been relegated to foundation plantings and nothing else. We need to be

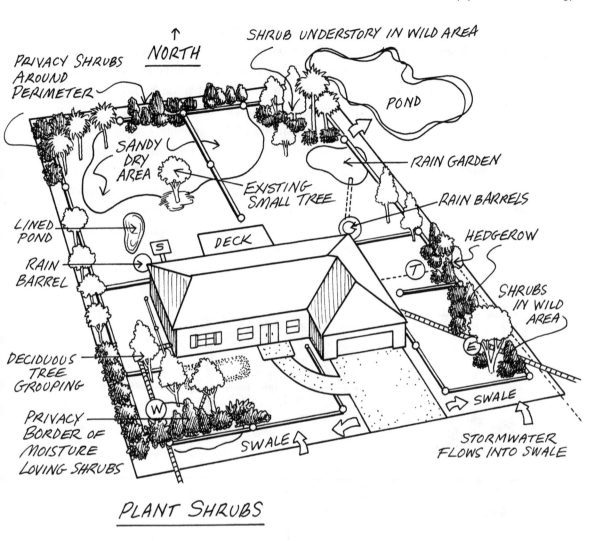

PRIVACY SHRUBS AROUND PERIMETER

↑ NORTH

SHRUB UNDERSTORY IN WILD AREA

POND

SANDY DRY AREA

RAIN GARDEN

EXISTING SMALL TREE

RAIN BARRELS

LINED POND

DECK

RAIN BARREL

S

T

HEDGEROW

SHRUBS IN WILD AREA

DECIDUOUS TREE GROUPING

E

PRIVACY BORDER OF MOISTURE LOVING SHRUBS

W

SWALE

SWALE

STORMWATER FLOWS INTO SWALE

PLANT SHRUBS

more imaginative and use shrubs in more places in the landscape because they can provide good habitat values including dense cover and food for wildlife.

As Foundation Plants

Sadly, the vast majority of the traditionally planted foundation shrubs are planted for instant curb appeal with no thought of how they'll look five or ten years later. They are planted too close together and too close to the house to accommodate their mature sizes. This means that after a few years, the shrubs will need severe pruning to keep them controlled to a reasonable size and to maintain an open view from the windows in your house. Overgrown foundation shrubs that are native or noninvasive alien species could be transplanted for use elsewhere in the landscape. Depending on how overgrown they are, the success rate may not be all that high, but you don't have anything to lose by trying except water, time, and energy. Keep in mind that the nonnative shrubs such as the widely planted Asian azaleas provide cover but add little else to the landscape's habitat values, so maybe a better use for them is to make compost or to add them to stick piles.

Foundation shrubs should be naturally small and slow growing, such as coonties or shiny blueberries. While you wait for them to grow to their mature sizes, you could plant groups of bunching grasses or other herbaceous plants with some structure between them. Maybe you could skip the shrubs for those restricted spaces altogether and plant a mixture of mostly perennial herbaceous plants with a variety of blooming times and year-round seasonal interest—a cottage garden. See Step 5 for ideas on herbaceous foundation plantings.

SHRUBS CAN REDUCE ENERGY USE

To Reduce Energy Bills

Strategically placed shrubs can help reduce the cost of your air conditioning by shading the condenser unit and by cooling the air through transpiration. If the unit is surrounded by hardscape, shrubs in large containers can provide shading and cooling.

Tall shrubs planted near the west or south walls of a building will also reduce air conditioning needs, and if the shrubs are deciduous, they will let filtered sun in during the winter months to reduce heating costs.

As Understory Plants

Whether you are creating a new grove as described in Step 3 or adding a shrub layer to an area where one or more trees are already growing, it's important to group the shrubs together by general size. Like trees, they'll look most natural if you plant them in groups of odd numbers and choose specimens that differ in height and branching patterns. If the yard is small, limit the number of shrub species for a more unified appearance. When planting shrubs under and around established trees, try to avoid cutting into major tree roots. Move the shrubs to places where you won't damage the tree roots when you dig planting holes. This may mean that the shrubs will be farther away from the trunks of the trees.

Adding to a New Grove

The understory plants set the tone or the feel of a new grove where one or more young trees have already been planted. It could be light and breezy with good visibility between the trees if the shrubs are low or it could be a dense thicket if you use a collection of tall shrubs around the trees. Decide what kind of grove would be most suitable for that location before choosing which shrubs to plant.

First, determine where the "front," or the most viewed, side of the grove is. It may be on the street side or it may be on the house side; in some cases it might be viewed from both sides. You'll want to arrange the shrubs to show off the layering of the trees and shrubs on the exposed sides to create depth and interest. Mark the edge of the projected mature canopy of the grove or the eventual drip line. The grove will look more natural if its edge is not circular or oval but more like the shape of an amoeba. If you are leaving some lawn that will still need to be mowed, create easily mowable edges (with no vertical barriers) and gentle curves. This way the mower can make a single clean sweep around the grove and will not have to come back with a trimmer to finish off the job. Some people add pavers set just above the level of the lawn, while others add mostly buried edging to keep the roots and rhizomes of the lawn plants from spreading into the grove.

Arrange the shrubs while they are still in their pots in groupings from just inside the drip line outward, keeping in mind how the whole arrangement will look from the most important vantage points. Some people also plant the larger herbaceous plants such as bunching grasses when they plant the shrubs, so include these plants too. As you did with the trees, walk around the arranged plants, take photos from different angles, and walk and talk through the arrangement with other members of your household and/or gardening friends to clarify what you are trying to accomplish with this round of planting.

Adding Understory to Lawn Trees

Adding shrub and herbaceous layers to build a grove around a single lawn tree or between two or more lawn trees is a relatively easy way to create more habitat and reduce the size of your lawn. Lawn trees are common in Florida landscaping; often one or more trees are planted in the middle of the front lawn.

Follow the steps listed above for a new grove, but there are a few extra issues to deal with when adding an understory.

- Find out the preferred conditions for the lawn tree and choose shrubs that also prefer those conditions. For instance, a southern magnolia (a common lawn tree even though it drops its leathery leaves year round) prefers slightly acidic soil and relatively dry conditions, so choose wild blueberries, native azaleas, inkberries, saw palmettos, or other shrubs that enjoy the same conditions and those magnolia leaves will become mulch in your new grove. But if your lawn tree is a sweetbay magnolia, which likes a wetter and more acidic environment, create a rain garden near the tree and direct the closest downspout to your new grove. Be careful not to dig a swale too close to the tree, but you could add a berm on the low side of the tree. Choose shrubs and other plants that are recommended for rain gardens. See Step 2 for ideas for rain gardens.
- If the lawn had been treated with pesticides and fertilizer, it's best to wait six weeks before starting this project. Stop these treatments on the remaining lawn because a successful bird and butterfly habitat depends on not using any landscape-wide poisons. (See Step 5 for more information on freedom lawns.)
- Size the planting area to be at least as large as the tree's leaf-drop area, which would be at least several feet outside the drip line. If the tree is in the exact center of the yard, it's a good idea to make the clearing larger on one side; you could plant the taller shrubs there. This off-center arrangement works best when the taller shrubs are on the far side of the tree from the front door or some other focal point in the landscape.

- It's best to remove the lawn manually to minimize disturbance to the tree's roots. Yes, this is hard work, but other options for lawn removal, such as using a herbicide or using cardboard with a heavy mulch layer on top, may damage the tree. Depending on how thick the lawn cover is, you may be able to use a turf cutter, cultivator, or iron rake to pull it out instead of digging it out with a shovel. However you remove the turf, leave as much soil as possible in place and remove as much as possible from the grass roots. Some types of grass such as St. Augustine may be dried and then added to the compost pile, but don't add weeds that might add seeds or those that can survive composting and continue to grow.
- Be careful not to damage the tree's large surface roots when digging the planting holes for your shrubs. Most established trees can tolerate some root damage, but work to reduce the damage while digging. Also, it's important to reduce the foot traffic while working under these trees.

The trees will do much better with a shrub layer around their roots than with lawn because of the reduced foot traffic and the cooler temperatures that the shrubs will create. These lawn tree thickets will become attractive working ecosystems that will require less and less maintenance as they mature.

Creating Understory Layers Next to an Established Wooded Area

A grouping of shrubs at the edge of a wooded area provides both a visual transition between the trees and the rest of the landscape and an extended habitat area to serve a wider range of wildlife. Also, it's better for the trees not to have to compete with lawn and withstand foot traffic. Use the same care when installing the shrubs as you would if you were installing a lawn tree grove. Planting taller shrubs closer to the trees and shorter ones closer to the edge creates layers. If possible, depending on the size and shape of the lot, plant some wider transition areas so the edge won't be a straight line. The wider areas could include a butterfly garden or a meadow-like area near its edge. (See Step 5 for butterfly gardens.)

Creating a Neat Edge for a Meadow or Wild Area

In some neighborhoods, a meadow may be mistaken for an overgrown lawn or a field of weeds. This may not conform to the expected landscape standards. One way to overcome some of the objections is to plant a neat shrub border with a clearly defined and mulched mowing edge. This edge gives the perception that the landscape is designed and tended.

MEADOW

SHRUBS

MAKE A NEAT BORDER

As with any other planting, plan for the mature size of the shrubs. At first they may not block out the view of the meadow, but you could add bunching grasses or showy container gardens between the shrubs until the shrubs mature. In most cases, choose shrub species that grow slowly but still fill out. They may also need to be trimmed to keep them neat.

On the other hand, if you have room, you could build a tall hedgerow at the edge of the meadow. This would require larger shrubs and small trees. A hedgerow would need very little trimming. See below for hedgerows.

Grouping Together as a Thicket

Shrub-only thickets can be built anywhere in the landscape to serve a variety of purposes.

- To make rain gardens more absorbent. Because of their larger size, when shrubs are used in rain gardens, they will absorb more water than herbaceous plants.
- To populate wild areas in back corners of small yards. Shrubs play an important part in adding habitat values, especially if they are chosen to provide flowers, berries, and dense cover at various levels of vegetation from the soil to just under the tree canopy. See Step 6 for more information on building wild areas in your landscape.
- As a wind-tolerant interruption of a wide expanse. Think of these as islands in a sea-like meadow where a shrub thicket could serve as a focal point to that section of the landscape. A thicket in a wide expanse will disrupt the air flows and could moderate wind damage during high-wind events.
- As a backdrop for a landscape feature such as a water feature or a butterfly garden. Shrubs provide important cover for birds and butterflies and will increase your wildlife traffic to these areas.
- As a privacy screen when grouped together as a hedgerow.

As a Hedgerow for Screening

Many Florida homes on small lots are close to other houses. Tall monoculture hedges such as Ficus or Australian pine are often seen in South Florida. Such hedges require a lot of trimming because these plants are full-sized trees. Also, because these hedges are created with only one plant species, they are at risk of dying out if they are infested with a pest or succumb to a disease.

A hedgerow serves a similar function to a hedge, but it is built with a variety of compatible shrubs or small trees planted in a zigzag pattern that leaves enough room so their projected mature sizes will overlap slightly. This zigzag pattern may need to be quite shallow for small properties so the hedgerow will not take up too much room as it matures.

Use at least three different species of shrubs or small trees, but more is recommended if you have room. Each species should be chosen for its texture and seasonal interest to be attractive you and to wildlife that will be looking for food in the form of berries, nectar, and leaves. Plant the small trees and taller shrubs toward the back of the hedgerow, but group several of the same species together to avoid a checkerboard pattern and to keep it more natural looking. A mature hedgerow will be lumpier and more interesting than a "normal" trimmed monoculture hedge, plus it will provide many more ecosystem services.

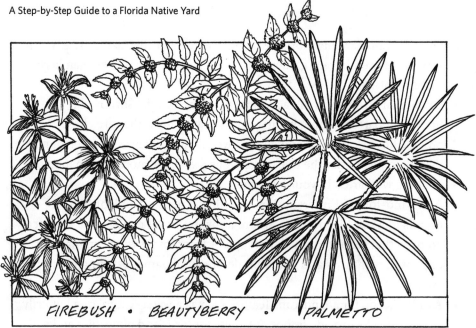

FIREBUSH • BEAUTYBERRY • PALMETTO

USE LEAF TEXTURE TO ADD INTEREST

A properly planned hedgerow has a number of advantages:

- It will need very little trimming since each shrub will be planted so that it can take its own shape and follow its normal growth pattern but will be planted close enough to other shrubs to provide good privacy screening.
- A hedgerow provides excellent cover for wildlife, and with the right mix of species it also can provide food such as berries and nectar all year round.
- Different shrubs species have their own seasonal interest. For instance, beautyberry will have showy berries from late summer through fall, native azalea has early spring blooms, an evergreen East Palatka holly has winter berries, and an oakleaf hydrangea has late spring flowers and fall color.
- Since the hedgerow will have different species, if one becomes infested with a pest or a disease, the rest of the plants will continue to provide screening and other benefits, unlike the monoculture hedges that can be completely wiped out if a disease hits.
- A tall hedgerow can act as a buffer to suppress sounds so even an urban landscape feels more peaceful.

- A dense hedgerow does a good job of cooling the immediate surroundings, so the space inside the hedge will be more comfortable than a sparsely planted landscape.
- The variety of textures in a good hedgerow will disrupt winds and help reduce the dust, including airborne pollutants, in your landscape. This wind shadow can be up to ten times longer than the height of the hedge, depending on the severity of the wind and other factors. A seven-foot-tall hedge provides protection for seventy feet.

SHRUBS OFFER FLEXIBLE CHOICES IN YOUR LANDSCAPE

Tall or short, wide or narrow, evergreen or deciduous, summer blooms or winter berries: shrubs provide versatile choices for your landscape and a good array of habitat values.

STEP 5

Working with Herbaceous Plants

While the woody plants in a landscape give it structure, often it is the herbaceous plants that determine its character. A landscape can appear to be messy or managed to a casual observer based solely on which species of herbaceous plants were planted (or allowed) and how they are maintained. You may see your landscape as a lovely butterfly haven, but your homeowners' association may object to your moth- and butterfly-eaten landscape. The neighborhood situation will be part of what you consider as you decide how to approach your herbaceous plantings. The default landscape expectations usually include a highly managed lawn; seasonal plantings of blooming pansies, impatiens, begonias, or mums; and severely clipped hedges and other shrubs. A mostly native landscape is usually more informal, subtler, and not in full bloom all the time. The good news is that public gardens like New York City's High Line park are changing people's perceptions and expectations of what beautiful landscapes look like.

There are three types of herbaceous plants:

- Annuals, which normally last one year and then die.
- Biennials, which store up energy, usually in a fat taproot, in their first season and then bloom in the second.
- Perennials, which can last from only a few years to decades. They usually die back during the winter and send up new growth each year.

In Florida's climate, plants sometimes behave differently, especially in frost-free zones. For instance, some perennials may not die back in the winter, biennials may go through their whole life cycle in one year, and annuals could last for several seasons. For designing purposes, it's best to include long-lived perennials because of their relative permanence. The goal of a mostly self-sustaining land-

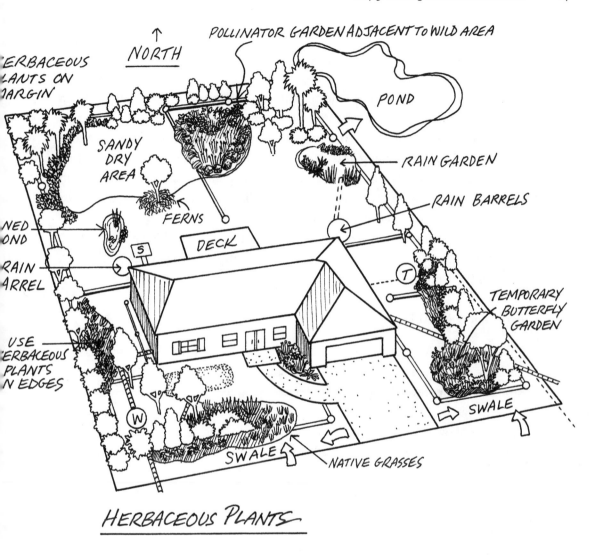

HERBACEOUS PLANTS ON MARGIN

↑ NORTH

POLLINATOR GARDEN ADJACENT TO WILD AREA

POND

SANDY DRY AREA

RAIN GARDEN

FERNS

RAIN BARRELS

NED OND

DECK

RAIN ARREL

S

T

TEMPORARY BUTTERFLY GARDEN

USE HERBACEOUS PLANTS N EDGES

W

SWALE

SWALE

NATIVE GRASSES

HERBACEOUS PLANTS

scape is incompatible with seasonal plantings, so you'd probably want to avoid plants that need to be replanted each year. Self-seeding annuals and short-lived perennials are useful in native areas to fill out the landscape while the perennials become established, although after the first season they could pop up unpredictably. Even though some of these desirable natives could become weedy, you could transplant the inconveniently self-planted specimens to better locations to begin another native area.

Because herbaceous plants are relatively small, short lived, and easy to transplant, you have much more freedom to rearrange them than woody plants, especially trees.

BROAD CATEGORIES OF HERBACEOUS PLANTS

Bunching Grasses or Grass-Like Plants

Bunching grasses and rushes tend to expand over the years but not spread via runners or rhizomes, although some will reseed. They can be planted in groupings, by themselves, or as the lower transition plants around the edge of a grove of trees or shrubs. Bunching grasses can serve as a low hedge when planted in a double row or tight zigzag line. They are suitable plants to substitute for turf in that awkward space between streets and sidewalks. Some are useful for ditches or rain gardens and some are salt tolerant.

There are a number of native, hardy, and easy-to-grow bunching grasses. These include muhly grass, Fakahatchee grass, bluestem grasses, lovegrasses, soft rushes, and many more.

Ferns and Fern Allies

These are primitive, nonflowering plants that produce spores and have an alternate life stage that is generally overlooked. The stage we are familiar with is the one that produces the spores—the sporophyte stage.

Ferns can be bunching or spreading. Some ferns die back in the winter, while others are showy all year round, especially in South Florida. Most ferns do well in shady damp areas, but some are adaptable to sunnier and drier spots. It's tempting to plant ferns under trees because most of them tolerate shade, but depending on the tree species, it can get quite dry near a tree because of the great volume of water that trees move out of the soil through transpiration.

Some good bunching ferns for Florida are cinnamon, royal, and leather ferns. Spreading ferns include netted chain fern and bracken. A commonly available fern ally is the scouring rush or horsetail, a moisture-loving spreading plant.

Wildflowers (Forbs)

There are many wonderful choices for Florida landscapes in this category. Remember that Ponce de León named our region La Florida (Land of the Flowers) more than 500 years ago because of our beautiful native flora. There are many ways to use wildflowers in your landscape, from edges and borders to meadows and butterfly gardens. Many of those sold in the native plant trade are short-lived perennials or self-seeding annuals, but a few will last much longer in the right conditions. Some can grow to two or three feet tall, but most are shorter than that.

Some good choices for taller wildflowers that can hold their own among bunching grasses are goldenrods, blazing stars, rosinweed, some species of milkweed, some sunflowers, spotted beebalm, and scarlet sage. Shorter flowers include Indian blanket, blue-eyed grass, black-eyed Susan, rain lilies, meadow garlic, tickseeds, and many more.

Ground Covers

Low-growing plants play a big role as ground covers in landscapes, especially in areas where you've removed lawn but you still want to retain the appearance or openness of a lawn. The most effective ground covers spread aggressively via rhizomes or runners (stolons). Use them as permanent plantings in areas where you need visibility or use them temporarily in areas between newly planted saplings.

While mulch is an important component of your developing native landscape, it should not be a dominant feature, because managing bare mulch in Florida will become an unending maintenance chore as weeds will grow on the surface and from under the mulch layer. So fill the open, non-lawn areas with ground covers to keep the weeds down or to at least make them seem less noticeable.

Some great ground covers include dune sunflower, frog fruit, sunshine mimosa, and wet twinflower.

Vines

Vines grow quickly and have many uses in a mostly native yard. They can be used on trellises or pergolas to provide quick shade and screening in a tight space. Vines can scramble up well-established trees or snags to provide cover and food for wildlife. Some vines are woody and long lasting, while others are herbaceous and sometimes die back in the winter. Most vines are easy to grow once they are established, but some can be quite aggressive, covering or shading tree foliage, so you need to keep track of what they are doing in the canopy.

Some of the woody vines that grow well in Florida are trumpet creeper, grape, Virginia creeper, and cross vine. Herbaceous vines include passionvine, coral honeysuckle, and Carolina jessamine. Be aware that some vines are quite aggressive in a managed landscape, so use with care.

SELECTING HERBACEOUS PLANTS

You can save money by buying seeds or small herbaceous plants, but larger specimens of herbaceous plants will have an immediate impact in the landscape. Using large herbaceous plants does not have the same downside that planting larger trees does because they usually establish easily and have a high rate of survival. (See Step 3 for the discussion of the benefits of using young saplings.)

Buy Locally Grown Seeds and Plants

The more local plants are, the better their chance of surviving Florida's climate. If you buy seeds, you can increase the germination rate by planting them in flats or large pots until the seedling stage so you will recognize them and can keep track of when they need water at this most vulnerable stage. When you plant these seedlings into your landscape, you will have better control of their placement than you would if you direct seeded. Extra irrigation will be needed for a couple of weeks until the plants are established.

Buy Plants and Seeds That Have Not Been Treated with Systemic Insecticides

A good way to avoid poisons is to support local native nurseries and native plant sales. Sometimes growers that supply big garden centers use systemic insecticides (mostly neonicotinoids) so the plants won't be eaten by caterpillars or other bugs and so they will continue to look good on the shelf. The systemic insecticides reside in every part of the plant, so long after they've been planted that they will continue to poison both the pollinators and the herbivores such as caterpillars. We want our plants to be more than just pretty; they should become part of the local ecosystem. We cheer when caterpillars eat our plants, so we don't poison them.

Separate Out Individual Plants If You Purchase a Large Container of Them

This way you have better control of the placement and the plants will have room to expand fully. This will save you money because you'll end up with a large number of plants now and it will save you time down the road because you won't need to separate them out for at least several years.

Avoid Specimens That Are Overly Root Bound

If the pot needs to be cut away to extract the plant(s), then it's root bound and less likely to thrive without extra care. If you end up with root-bound plants, spend extra time soaking the root ball and divide the bunch into at least three chunks so there will be places for new growth to occur. Do not trim the tops of the plants because the hormones produced by the terminal buds encourage root growth. After planting these stressed plants, irrigate liberally for an extended period of time to increase the likelihood that they will survive.

PLANTING HERBACEOUS PLANTS

Rinsing all the soil away from the root ball is not necessary as recommended for trees and shrubs, but it is a good idea to disturb the roots to some extent. One of the best strategies is to cut the bottom half of the root ball in quarters from the bottom of the root ball and then spread out the bottom-most roots like wings so they are near the soil surface when they are placed in the planting hole. For larger plants, it's best to mud them into their planting holes so the root ball is soaked. In most cases do not add any amendments to the planting hole, but you could add a top dressing of compost to the whole planting area to revitalize the soil with new microbes. Add mulch around the plants (over the compost) to deter weeds, moderate temperature fluctuations, and keep in the moisture. Irrigate every day for a week or so until the plants no longer wilt in the heat of the day.

In most cases, it's a good idea to arrange herbaceous plants in drifts in a meadow or a butterfly garden so they will have a larger impact visually. Also, planting similar plants together simplifies the ongoing maintenance because they can all be treated the same. It's also been shown that related plants sometimes build below-ground communications through mycorrhizae soil fungi.

LAWNS TO MEADOWS

For far too long, Americans have had a love affair with their lawns, especially in Florida. People spend a lot of time and money on their unsustainable lawn care. The default Florida lawn-care regimen is to buy sod, usually various cultivars of St. Augustine or Zoyzia, irrigate heavily until established, pay people to come poison the grass to keep out weeds and bugs, and then fertilize it because the soil is weakened from the harsh treatment. In the winter, the turf grass goes dormant because it is our dry season and the days are cooler and shorter. The dormant grass is overseeded with a winter grass (usually winter rye), which then needs to be watered heavily (during our dry season) to get it started. This means that the lawn needs mowing throughout the year.

Despite all the time and money poured into such a lawn, it is likely to fail within a few years. Homeowners will pay big bucks to resod the whole lawn to start the whole process again, thinking that somehow this time it will succeed. The definition of insanity is doing the same thing repeatedly expecting a different outcome. Isn't it time to stop this madness?

Vignette: A Lawn-Free Native Yard Is Possible in a Homeowners' Association

A couple moved into a home in a large retirement village on a small lot of one-tenth of an acre in Central Florida. They have broken the mold for their neighborhood. Instead of allowing the management company to maintain the original, mostly lawned landscape, they maintain the landscape themselves. They've replaced all of the lawn with native trees, shrubs, vines, and herbaceous plants from bunching grasses to ground covers. They also built a rain garden and in a different section brought in some sand to simulate a beach and a pathway. They have used more than fifty different plant species, which is a lot for such a small landscape, but they have grouped species into organized mass plantings and have divided the landscape into small sections with paths and stepping-stones, so the large number of different species seems organized and calming. Their lush native plants bordering the edges of the yard make their neighbors' yards seem so boring.

They worked with their homeowners' association and have kept the wilder plants trimmed back, so it's the tidiness of the whole landscape (especially the herbaceous plants) that stands out. This cooperation within the community provides some lessons for others. They have started a chapter of the Florida Native Plant Society in their community that has attracted many members. They have received good publicity for their efforts and provide yard tours for Master Gardeners and other local groups. Now an increasing number of fellow residents are following suit with their own mostly native yards.

The key here is that this landscape is maintained to the expected aesthetic of the community so that no one would mistake it for a bunch of weeds. It offers good habitat values for birds and butterflies for such a small lot and is also quite beautiful. These are the reasons why this native landscape is accepted in a highly managed community.

Freedom Lawns

The process of transforming your yard to create habitat for birds and butterflies is incompatible with the pesticide and fertilization applications and overseeding regimens used by most lawn-care companies. You may decide to keep some lawn spaces in your yard, but without the unsustainable lawn care, on a permanent or

FREEDOM LAWN

TURFGRASS
(MONOCULTURE)

LOW GROWING HERBACEOUS PLANTS CREATE
DIVERSITY IN A FREEDOM LAWN

temporary basis depending on the timeline of your plans, your family's needs, and your neighborhood. When you discontinue this type of lawn care, be prepared for an adjustment period where the grass is allowed to go dormant and some patches of turf may die back.

To help the lawn and its underlying soil recover during this withdrawal process, mow the lawn with a low cut—maybe two inches. After the close mowing, thoroughly rake the thatch from the turf using a flexible leaf rake. Add the dead thatch material to your compost. It's fine to do this in sections because it's a lot of work.

After you dethatch your lawn, apply a thin layer of fine, locally made compost (with no manures) over the whole yard in early spring on a dry day when no heavy storms are expected. Lightly irrigate the area so the compost is washed from the blades of grass and makes contact with the soil, but make sure that none of the water flows from the lawn. You could repeat the compost boost the following spring as well, but after that, the soil will probably be recovered enough from all the pesticide treatments and will be better able to support your lawn plants.

New plants will eventually fill in the dead patches, but you could plant ground covers or sow some wildflower seeds in those bare spots to hurry the transformation. A good freedom lawn will be filled with many species of plants that tolerate mowing.

The ongoing care of a freedom lawn includes mowing at the highest setting on your mower, usually four inches. Mow only when needed, so you may not have to mow at all from November to March, when the grass goes dormant. But if there is significant leaf drop during this dormant time, you could use the mower to mulch the leaves in place or gather up some of the chopped leaves to add to your compost pile. Cut way back on the irrigation and make sure the irrigation system is turned off when there has been significant rainfall. You may need to irrigate your lawn areas only three or four times a year when there has been significant drought during the growing season.

After a few years, there may still be some of the original turf grass left, but the freedom lawn will host a wide variety of other plants that will have come in on their own. You'll probably notice that birds, butterflies, and many other pollinators will be enjoying your lawn plants as well. You will have made Mother Nature happy and just think of all the money you'll save. (See the butterfly garden section below for more information on poisons.)

Meadows

To start a meadow, you can just stop mowing a whole section of lawn, you can remove the lawn a little at a time around the edges, or you could kill all the grass with a thick layer of mulch. Your situation will determine the most logical method of meadow creation. If there are neighborhood regulations or expectations, it may be more comfortable to replace the lawn a little at a time. Your landscaping timeline may call for a plan to work on other areas first and then eventually transform the lawn.

The cessation of mowing is the easiest way to start a meadow. This action may be problematic in neighborhoods with landscaping rules. In such cases, you can work to make the lawn look more civilized by creating a neat, mulched edge of shrubs or bunching grasses or by mowing a curving path through it that leads to a bench. Planting areas of wildflowers in the former lawn will break up the initial grassy plant mix with splashes of color. Each year add drifts of wildflowers in different areas until you reach an attractive ratio of grasses to wildflowers. It's best to remove some of the more aggressive pioneer plants such as Spanish needles that tend to dominate meadows at first. In addition, if there are trees nearby, tree seedlings will need to be removed if you wish the meadow to persist. Some people take care of tall weeds and trees by mowing the area once a year in the winter at the highest level possible on the mower. For smaller areas use a weed whacker or a string trimmer and cut at six inches.

If the lawn is removed or smothered, plant the meadow area as soon as possible; otherwise the most aggressive weeds will take over. Even if most of the plants will

---

Vignette: Lawn Reduction

A couple bought a relatively new home in North Florida on a 1.5-acre lot. The previous owner had sodded most of the landscape, which was mostly outlined by a mature wooded fringe. One of the sodded areas, about one-tenth of an acre, had not been prepared well for turf and was difficult to mow. It was located where there was no need for grass and was surrounded by trees, so the homeowners stopped mowing.

Grass, tree seedlings, and many other types of plants grew tall, so for several years the homeowners used a weed whacker to cut down the tall weeds. They also pulled or dug out the trees to maintain the plot as a meadow. They also created a mulched path through the area just inside one of the rows of trees. Then one year, they stopped cutting it back in the winter and trees started to take over. They continued to maintain the path and later selectively removed the trees in one much smaller area. They added a few native azaleas and hollies plus a few other selected natives that provide food and shelter for birds.

In the end, the lawn was replaced by a mostly wooded area that has become its own ecosystem that supports many bird species and butterflies and other wildlife. The ongoing maintenance includes occasional removal of invasive plants, keeping the small area as a meadow, and applying more wood chips on the path every other year or so.

They also allowed some other large areas of lawn in their landscape to grow out to become meadows, woods, or a combination of both. The total lawn area is about one-third of its original size. The lawn that is left looks as green as their neighbors' yards most of the time, even though it has been a freedom lawn for more than ten years.

be introduced via seed, you could create initial structure with some started plants in strategic locations. If you'll be purchasing plants, arrange them in groupings and don't leave too much space between them. You can save money by purchasing smaller plants or seedlings. Be sure to irrigate enough so your plants or new seedlings can establish themselves.

PERENNIALS AS FOUNDATION PLANTINGS

All too often, young specimens of large shrubs are used as foundation plantings. While they may look okay when first planted, just a few years later they may need severe pruning to keep them from blocking windows and growing into walkways. As mentioned in Step 4, if you're lucky, they will be native shrubs that could be used elsewhere in your landscape. Otherwise, it's best to just dig them out and start over.

This time, instead of planting another set of shrubs, create a perennial garden that includes a variety of plants that have varied seasonal interest and won't outgrow the space. Choose plants that provide year-round structure as the backbone species, such as coonties or bunching grasses. Then plant other perennials or self-seeding annuals in groupings in front of or in between your main structure plants. Be sure to mulch the area well to deter the weeds to some extent. It won't be maintenance free, but the degree of tidiness is up to you and depends on your situation. This area could be set up as a butterfly garden and the grass and wildflower seeds could feed the birds, so don't be too quick to deadhead the spent flowers. Watching the birds and butterflies flitting around your house will be so much more rewarding than looking at the back of overgrown shrubs. (See below for more details on butterfly gardens.)

CONTAINER GARDENS

Most container gardens are populated by herbaceous plants, but you could also use small shrubs as part of the mix of plants. Containers are useful in a developing landscape because they are mobile and can serve as fillers or focal points among trees or shrubs that have not matured yet. Container gardens can be used in paved areas or as borders along the edges of patios or decks. Many people like to have several different types of container gardens that can be cycled in and out of prominent locations, depending on whether they are blooming or showy in another way.

Use the largest containers that are practical for your situation so you can relocate them without too much strain. A dolly is helpful for handling large containers. The large volume of soil will provide better conditions for your plants: there will be more room for the roots and there will be less temperature and moisture fluctuations.

To build a container garden, lay in leaves, pine needles, straw, or weed-barrier cloth in the bottom to keep the soil from running out the drainage holes. Do not use a layer of gravel or potsherds because they actually impede drainage. Use taller pots for the best drainage. Add a mixture of garden soil and compost up to a few inches below the rim. (If you don't have compost, use bagged organic soil that has rested for at least a few days in direct contact with your soil, possibly mixed with some leaves.) Then install your plants and cover the soil with mulch. Some people treat containers like bouquets with three levels of plants—tall (the thriller), medium (the filler), and low, overhanging plants (the spiller). Also, a container planted with a single species can then be arranged with containers planted with a different plant species in pleasing ways.

Containers will need irrigation even after the plants are established, so either vow to water by hand on a regular basis, especially on hot days, or install an automatic or semi-automatic drip irrigation system for all your containers. A drip irrigation system is more trouble to set up but less trouble in the long run and your containers will be much more successful.

Containers can also be used for edible crops. You can move them to sunny areas in the winter, but maybe move them to slightly shadier locations as the weather gets hotter. Edible crops will need a richer soil mixture with more nutrients than natives. They also will produce a better harvest if the moisture is constant. Use an automatic drip irrigation system or self-watering containers with a water reservoir in the bottom that is wicked up into the soil.

For long-term containers, add half an inch of top dressing of compost two or three times a year, especially just before the growing season for that plant (or plants). This will rejuvenate the soil's microbes and provide a gentle boost of nutrients. Remulch the exposed soil.

BUTTERFLY GARDENS

Butterfly gardens need to be located in mostly sunny, unpoisoned areas. They are planted with a wide variety of flowers to attract adult butterflies and other pollinators plus host plants to feed the butterfly larvae—the caterpillars. Herbaceous butterfly gardens fill in quickly and are good starting project for your native landscaping. You may wish to locate some butterfly gardens near a window or deck so you and your family can enjoy the flying menagerie. If you start your garden with at least some purchased plants (rather than planting everything from seed), your

PLANT A WIDE VARIETY OF HERBACEOUS PLANTS—
TO ATTRACT POLLINATORS

butterfly garden will take shape even more quickly and begin to attract pollinators right away.

A butterfly garden may be planted as a permanent landscape feature or it can be installed as a temporary arrangement to fill in an empty spot. One typical temporary location would be where you've planted a grouping of tree saplings spaced out for their mature sizes. Later, when those trees start to produce significant shade, start a new butterfly garden in a different sunny spot—maybe a new space to replace some more lawn. (See Step 3.)

While butterflies are the headliners for this type of garden, it will be popular with other pollinators such as moths, bees, wasps, and even hummingbirds. On top of that, all the pollinators attracted to your garden will bring their predators such as toads, lizards, dragonflies, assassin bugs, praying mantises, and birds. Your butterfly garden will become the basis for a working ecosystem. So let's get started . . .

Don't Use Poisons

While it's obvious that you wouldn't spray poison on the butterflies or their larvae, there are some instances when the poisoning may be unintentional:

- Landscape-wide applications of pesticides

Most are done as part of the general lawn-care regimens to kill the mole crickets, webworms, imported red fire ants, and other pests that damage turf grass. Your butterfly garden will not be successful if you allow these broad-spectrum insecticides to be sprayed indiscriminately across your yard. Convert your turf grass to a freedom lawn by stopping the applications of insecticides, fungicides, herbicides, and fertilizers. You'll save money and your pesticide-free lawn will eventually host many different types of plants that tolerate mowing. (See above for more information on freedom lawns.)

- Systemic insecticides

Plants absorb these insecticides, usually neonicotinoids. The poison will be present throughout the plants, so when caterpillars and other herbivores eat the plants they will be poisoned. Even the pollen and nectar will be poisonous; this harms the pollinators as well. If you're buying plants to give your butterfly garden a head start, be sure that they are free from these systemic poisons. Some seed that you purchase may be coated with systemic insecticides, so watch out for that as well. In general, these insecticides are used so that plants will look good on the shelf.

- Homemade concoctions

Mixtures of household substances are often recommended as a "safe" way to kill pests whether they are weeds or insects such as aphids. Various soapy solutions are suggested as a way of killing aphids or whiteflies on your plants, but the soap will also kill other bugs that are predators of those pest insects. In addition, the soap will damage the waxy cuticle that coats and protects the plants from wilting, fungal attacks, and, yes, insect damage. Various vinegar solutions are recommended as weed killers, but if you spray a bunch of weeds, the vinegar will also kill the toads that may have been living in the weeds. In addition, vinegar changes the acidity of the soil, which may affect worms and other soil critters.

Consider the consequences of using anything that's toxic, organic or not, in your landscape. You want to encourage the predators of the pests, but when a pest is causing problems, you can take actions that do not involve poison, such as washing with water and hand picking. See the University of Florida's Extension Service resources on Integrated Pest Management (http://ipm.ifas.ufl.edu/).

Plant in Sunny Spots

Butterflies and most other pollinators are cold-blooded animals that are attracted to warm, sunny spots. In Florida, gardeners often strive to develop more shade in their landscapes to reduce the ambient heat around houses, to make it more pleasant to be outside, and to save money on air conditioning costs. But if you want butterflies, leave some sunny spots. To host as many butterflies as possible you might build more than one garden—one to catch the morning sun and another one that's sunny in the afternoon.

Choose plants that thrive in hot, sunny conditions and ones that will thrive in the normal moisture level of the soil in that area. Keep in mind that even if your spot is hot and dry and you've chosen plants that can withstand these conditions, you will still need to irrigate regularly until they are established.

Plant Masses of Plants

Experts say that many pollinators have poor eyesight and are attracted to large swaths of color. From a design viewpoint, so are humans. Depending on the size of your butterfly garden, massing may be limited to only a few sections. Avoid a checkerboard arrangement by planting several of one plant species together and then arrange several of the next plant species in the next open space. Keep the mature size of your plants in mind: plant the shorter ones near the edges and the taller ones behind them. If you're planting seeds, it usually a good idea to purchase packets of individual species rather than seed assortments. This way you have more control over the arrangement of the plants.

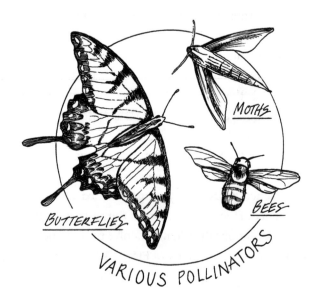

Vary the Flowers

Choose species of plants from different plant families to ensure that the flower types will vary in color, structure, and blooming time. Wide, compound flower heads like those in the daisy family and narrow tubular flowers like those in the mint family will provide habitat for pollinators with long proboscises and those with shorter ones. Choose your plants so that something is in bloom year round; there are often warm spells in our Florida winters that may cause some butterflies and other pollinators to emerge from dormancy early.

Plants that volunteer in the landscape demonstrate that they can survive there, and if they are native, they are candidates for inclusion in the butterfly gardens. If they are too aggressive, keep them trimmed back and confined to small sections.

Include Host Plants

A butterfly garden should include host plants for butterfly larvae. Most butterflies can drink nectar from a wide variety of flowers, but many are limited to only one type of host plant such as milkweed for monarchs and passionvine for gulf fritillaries and zebra longwings, our state butterfly. See below for resources for finding good host plants.

Real butterfly gardeners cheer when the caterpillars
appear in their landscapes.

Create Some Cover

Butterflies require some dense cover that can serve as shelter from the weather and predators in or near the butterfly garden. It's a good idea to locate your butterfly garden in an area that backs up to a grove, a hedgerow, or a wild area where at least some vegetation grows from the ground to the canopy. You can create some cover with a trellis or a pergola covered with vines near your butterfly garden. Some shrubs attract butterflies when they are in bloom and some are host plants. In addition, shrubs can provide good cover. So if possible include a group of butterfly-friendly shrubs near your butterfly gardens.

Provide Water and Mud

A water feature such as a pond with a trickle fountain and an exposed mud shoreline provides drinking water and a source of minerals. (See Step 2 for more information on building and maintaining ponds.)

HERBACEOUS PLANTS ARE MUCH MORE THAN SEASONAL PLANTINGS

Many "professionally landscaped" properties run through a cycle of seasonal plantings that provide full bloom all year round: pansies in the winter, begonias or impatiens in the summer, and mums in the fall. This strains your pocketbook, the soil, and your back. In addition, seasonal plantings do very little for the butterflies or the bees. So think of herbaceous plants as more permanent partners in your ecosystem building. They might not be in full bloom 100 percent of the time, but they will always be playing a part in your local ecosystem.

BUTTERFLY GARDEN RESOURCES

- "Butterfly Gardening in Florida" (http://edis.ifas.ufl.edu/uw057), an Extension Service resource that includes a long list of host plants for Florida's butterflies.
- The North American Butterfly Association website (http://butterflyassociation.org/) has ideas and resources, plus it can certify your yard as butterfly habitat.
- The Butterflies and Moths of North America website (http://www.butterfliesandmoths.org/) includes lists of both the favored nectar plants and host plants for each species of butterfly.

STEP 6

Build a Wild or Natural Area

Doug Tallamy has shown us that even small pockets of native plants provide significant habitat values, so set aside some wild places in your landscape. To work well as habitat, these areas should include foliage or other cover from the ground to the canopy. They should not be frequented by humans or pets or highly managed once they are established. Depending on the state of the landscape and the structure the wild area, it may take a number of years before the area matures enough to become a low-maintenance habitat, but the rewards are well worth the wait.

The National Wildlife Federation (www.nwf.org) says that good habitat should include food, shelter, water, and places for wildlife to raise their young. The NWF created a habitat certification program in 1973 that has been wildly popular: today, more than 200,000 spaces representing 1.5 million acres are Certified Wildlife Habitats in suburban yards, schools, campuses, corporate properties, farms, parks, and more. The certification process is a good exercise to go through, especially with kids at home or at a school. As part of the process, you may wish to purchase the certified habitat sign to display so that people passing by your yard will understand what you are doing with all your native plants and might be inspired to do the same. The NWF also certifies schools, communities, and other organizations with property that could be transformed from lawns to habitat. (See the introduction for a more complete discussion on this certification.)

In many cases the best places for wild areas are in back corners of your lot, where they are mostly out of sight and are not used by people or pets for their outdoor activities. But if the best places are more visible, you may need to guide the growth of your new wild space so that it never looks like a bunch of weeds to the neighbors. As previously discussed in this book, there are a number of ways to approach this problem such as making the changes a little at a time or creating a civilized edge with shrubs or bunching grasses that hide the interior area while the plants mature.

The goal of this area is to create a space that will eventually take care of itself with only minor maintenance around the edges. If you begin this project by pulling out lawn, all that newly exposed soil will attract weeds, so lay in a good layer of mulch such as pine needles or chipped wood on unplanted soil to reduce the weeds. Be sure that mulch does not touch the trunks of your trees or shrubs—leave a three- to six-inch gap. Keep the weeds pulled and refresh the mulch once a year for several years. Using this aggressive treatment up front means that you'll have fewer weeds to remove, which minimizes soil disturbances, which in turn leads to fewer weeds. Also, as the trees and shrubs mature, they'll cast more shade and become self-mulching with their own leaves and twigs, thus further reducing the need for maintenance. Your wild area will become wilder and its habitat values will increase as the years go by.

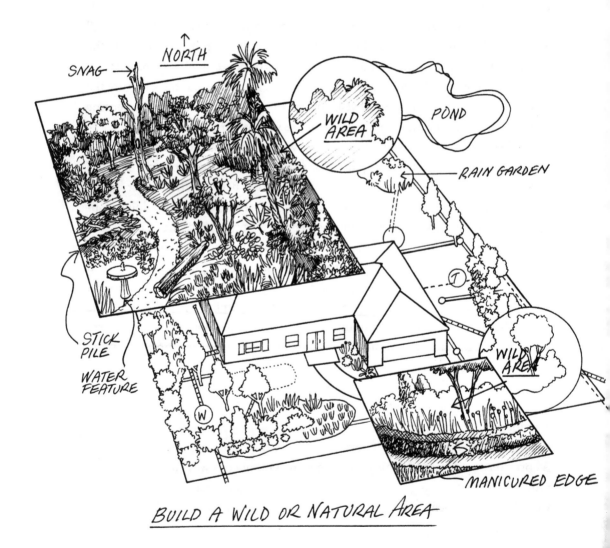

BUILD A WILD OR NATURAL AREA

CREATING WILD AREAS

The best method of creating a wild area will vary depending on the state of your yard. If you're lucky, you'll have mature native trees in appropriate places to serve as centerpieces for one or more wild areas. Existing trees will provide a big head start and you can build the natural area with other trees and shrubs that complement your existing trees. But you can still create a useful wild area on a cleared or lawned lot. It will just take a longer for it to become established and it will go through several stages along the way.

Since the goal of creating this space is to support wildlife, you may wish to place a few bird-oriented water features such as a few birdbaths of differing heights and a solar-powered trickle fountain with a recirculating water supply in the front of this space. The wild space would then become a backdrop for the decorative water features, so its wildness will tend to be less of a problem. Having nearby shelter means that birds can hop out for a bath or a drink and quickly retreat if there is a threat. Having a recirculating system means that you don't need to change the water every three days because the mosquito larvae will be filtered out. If you add rocks to form shallow spaces in part of this water feature, it will also attract butterflies and smaller birds. Having a pond next to your wild area will increase the habitat value even more, whether it's a small, preformed pond or a larger in-ground pond.

Whether you are starting with a blank slate or with established trees, it's a good idea to designate at least one out-of-the-way place in your wild area for a stick pile. Stick piles provide shelter for small birds and places for insects to overwinter or pupate into their next life cycle stage. Most people build stick piles in stages as they prune trees, pick up fallen branches, or cut back tall weeds. Plants with hollow stems are particularly useful. It's best not to disturb the pile once you start it—just add more material to the top to keep it going. The bottom material will eventually compost itself into the soil, but that's a good thing for toads and other soil critters looking for soft, sheltered places to hide. In addition, many native bees and predatory wasps create burrows in the soil, and the soil surface under the stick pile provides unplanted and unmulched spaces they can use.

Starting with a Cleared or Lawned Space

Decide whether the space is large enough and has enough vertical and horizontal growing room to support one or more full-sized trees. A grove of three or more full-sized trees would be ideal, but if you don't have the space, you can still create an effective wild space with a one tree, even a small one, surrounded by shrubs of

Build a stickpile for wildlife. Use shrubs to screen it from view.

different sizes; a grouping of small trees surrounded by tall shrubs; or a thicket of tall shrubs.

Choose woody plants with good habitat values:

- Evergreen cover year round, such as one of the hollies
- Food in the form of fruit or nuts, such as hickories or beautyberries
- Nectar plants and larval food for insects, such as cherries or oaks

If there is adequate vertical room for trees but limited horizontal space for the roots because of hard structures like sidewalks, driveways, or foundations, palms may be the best choice for the tree component of the wild area because palm roots do not expand like woody plants and will not disturb the nearby infrastructure. Consult Steps 3 and 4 for ideas and guidelines for choosing and planting trees and shrubs.

As you remove the lawn, plant a dense cover of bunching grasses, wildflowers, and ground covers around your woody plants while they are small. Add organic mulch such as wood chips or pine needles around your herbaceous plants to reduce the weed growth and the need to disturb the soil.

As discussed in Step 5, this area could be a temporary butterfly garden. Over the next few years as the trees and shrubs grow, there will be more shade and your understory plants will change to more shade-tolerant plants. You can let the plants die out naturally or you can hurry up the process by moving some of your initial, sun-loving plants such as bunching grasses outward as needed and installing shade-tolerant plants closer to the trees.

To give the area some initial structure, install some snags. You probably won't have any real dead trees in a cleared site, but you might have access to some logs or large branches that could serve the purpose. If you don't have any in your

MANY CREATURES CAN USE
WILD AREAS, EVEN IN A SMALL YARD

neighborhood, your county might have some available at a dump or you might call some tree services to ask for logs. Dig a hole that is deep enough to secure the log in its new vertical position. Deeper holes will be needed for sandy soil. If possible, use an odd number of snags and arrange them at different heights, like a flower arrangement. These fake snags will provide vertical accents and provide several habitat values while you are waiting for your trees to grow. You could add birdhouses at the tops of the snags, or if there is enough thickness, you could gouge or drill out various sized holes to create nesting sites. Planting vines at the bottom of each snag will increase the habitat value and will also make them more attractive in your landscape. Choose native vines with good habitat value such as coral honeysuckle, Virginia creeper, or native passionvines, which would provide nectar for hummingbirds and butterflies, berries for birds, and food for caterpillars. A tangle of vines also provides nesting sites and good cover.

As your planted trees grow taller, these snags may become more shaded, which is fine for their habitat values, but the sun-loving vines may not be so happy in the shade. You could take cuttings or train some of the vining stems along the ground out into sunnier areas and provide them with new snags or trellises to climb. Be careful digging around your new trees because you don't want to damage their roots. Surface roots of a healthy tree often spread 30 percent more than the height of the tree.

Starting with Established Trees or Tall Shrubs

One or more established trees will give you a big head start in building a wild area. True natives are the best, but nativar trees (cultivars of a native such as Little Gem magnolia) or nonnative trees could also be used to start a wild area, as long as they are noninvasive, such as crapemyrtle. Maybe you can plan to remove or kill the nonnative trees in a few years when your new native trees and shrubs grow enough to take their place in the canopy and offer good habitat values. If you girdle the nonnative tree by removing a three-inch strip of bark all the way around its trunk, it will die within a year and you'll have a snag, which will offer good habitat to your wild area. (Girdling does not work on palms.)

Wild areas can be formed around one or more lawn trees, as described in Step 4. A grouping is better, but habitat can be created around a single tree. In both cases, observe where the leaves drop. This leaf-drop space should be the minimum area for your wild space.

Arrange groupings of small trees and tall shrubs around the edges of the leaf-drop area. These shrubs should tolerate partly shaded areas and be compatible with

Ecotones

The transition area between two or three separate plant communities is called an ecotone. If you walk from a field into a mature forest, you'll have to fight through a tangle of shrubs, vines, and low branch growth on trees before you enter the true forest, where the ground is not heavily vegetated and the branches on most trees are high in the canopy. You have just experienced an ecotone. Ecotones, especially at the edges of wooded areas, support a higher density of organisms and a greater number of species than are found in either flanking community. Some organisms require a transitional area for activities such as courtship, nesting, or foraging for food.

the trees. For instance, if you have a group of pine trees, use acid-loving shrubs such as blueberry, holly, or azalea. Just think how nice it will be not to have to clear out all those pine needles from the lawn anymore!

Choose young shrub plants so they will adjust easily and quickly to their new surroundings without too much work on your part or too much damage to the roots of the existing trees. A mixture of evergreen and deciduous shrubs provides good habitat and good interest in your landscape.

Whether you start with existing trees or a cleared area, shrubs could form the edges of your wild space or you could add a low shrubs or herbaceous border outside the shrubs to act as a transition area between the wild area and its surroundings. This layer could be herbaceous; you could use bunching grasses, ferns, or meadow wildflowers or low shrubs such as coonties, low blueberries, or St. John's wort. You could also use this transition area as a more permanent butterfly garden. A transition layer provides a more gradual shift between the wooded area and the ground cover area—an ecotone that will provide better habitat for many small birds and other wildlife than a tall shrub-to-lawn interface.

If the space next to the wild area is a walkway or a lawn, the low transition layer will reduce the trimming needed for the shrubs at the edge of the wild area and make it feel less crowded, which is important for a small landscape. Walking and mowing next to the transition area will be easier as well.

Vignette: A Plant Community–Based Native Yard for Study and Learning

Instead of planning a landscape for purely aesthetic reasons, a coastal resident in South Florida decided to create several study gardens based on native Florida plant communities in his small yard.

He planned a subtropical hammock for the backyard. The hammock would wrap around a screened porch and patio, provide shade and wildlife value, and create a quiet and lush retreat in the middle of town.

Canopy trees to provide all-day shade were planted first, including paradise tree and pigeon plum. He planted bahama, smooth, and little strongbarks for their scented flowers and their ability to produce food for migrating songbirds. Wild coffee, lancewood, and marlberry provide a shrub understory, and coonties encourage the once-endangered Atala butterfly to take up residence.

As the hammock matured, leaf litter collected and created hiding and feeding places for animals like moles, glass lizards, and black racers. These species in turn fed on troublesome insects like roaches, eliminating the need for any kind of pest control. Leaf litter also replaced mowing and mulching in the backyard. Maintenance in the hammock area is simple: only occasional trimming and gathering of fallen branches is needed. Branches and trimmings are incorporated into a stick pile that provides shelter for various small creatures.

Pleased with the hammock, the owner decided to create three other study areas—a demonstration scrub garden in a hot, sandy area with no irrigation (the yard is in an area that once bordered a natural sand pine scrub), a small

WILD SPACE GOALS

The goal of a wild area is to become a low-maintenance and low traffic area that provides shelter and food for a variety of wildlife. While you could continue to add to the stick pile in your wild area, eventually the only maintenance you will need to do will be to remove bird-planted invasive plants in that space. Wild areas can also serve as screening or transition spaces, especially if your property backs up to a park, a right of way, or some other public property.

wetland of about 150 square feet, and a coastal strand featuring seagrape, dune sunflower, beach bean, sea oats, sea lavender, bay cedar, and more.

The scrub site has been the most difficult to establish. Some plants have not flourished. Plants in the scrub area include scrub oaks, sand pine, saw palmetto, blue curls, Chapman's blazing star, and large-flowered false rosemary, which successfully reseeded. Maintenance in the scrub area is somewhat high since constant hand pulling of weeds is required to keep the open patches of sand, which is characteristic of scrub habitat.

The wetland area has been a great success. A preformed kidney-shaped pond was set at ground level. The surrounding area was excavated and sloped, then a large pond liner was added over the entire area. The pond creates a deeper section that keeps fish and other small aquatic animals safe from predators, while the shallow areas allows places for invertebrates of various kinds to go about their business.

Once the wetland area was filled with water, the owner added a couple of five-gallon buckets of ditch water to the pond to introduce natural microorganisms, allowing the pond to quickly stabilize. A half-dozen mosquito fish were added to eat mosquito larvae, and the pond has become a haven for dragonflies, beetles, leopard frogs and snails. A pair of mottled ducks even visited for a brief time. Numerous native wetland plants like the scarlet hibiscus, white-topped sedge, pickerelweed, and yellow flag surround the edges of the pond and aquatic plants have colonized the wetter areas. The owner continues to be amazed at the number of species of animals this created wetland attracts to his yard.

STEP 7

Create Spaces for Human Use

When you replace wide expanses of lawn with trees and shrubs on your property, it will be cooler than the surrounding areas and will be filled with birds and butterflies. So why not plan to enjoy some time with family and friends outside? First

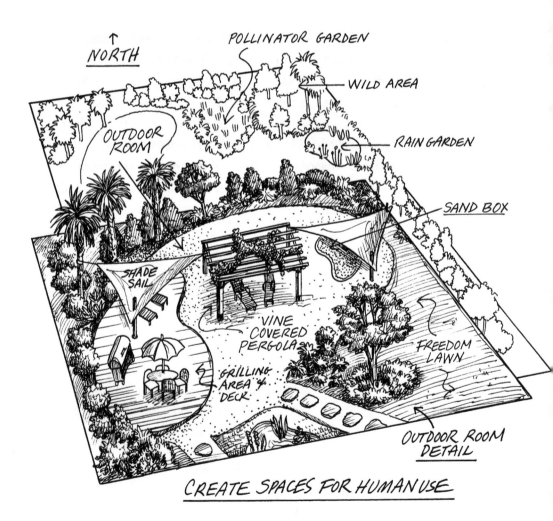

CREATE SPACES FOR HUMAN USE

make a list of all the potential uses for this space so you can create the best design for the surrounding landscape. Keep in mind that outside activities will change as your family's needs change.

OUTDOOR ROOMS

In a small landscape the space available for human uses will be limited, but you will set the mood for each space with the choices you make for three defining components for this space.

The Floor

If there will be furniture such as picnic tables, patio chairs and tables, and/or a gas or charcoal grill, plan for some type of decking or sturdy pavers to support the furniture and equipment. Be sure to choose a surface that will allow stormwater to soak in. If the area is prone to dampness, you could build a large dry well under the

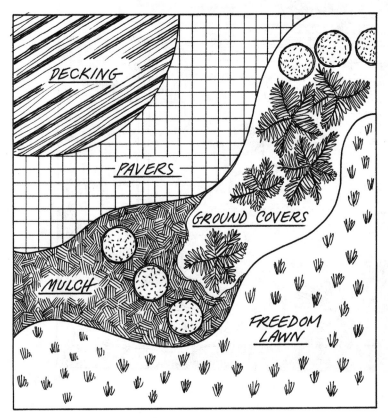

OUTDOOR ROOMS - FLOOR

pavers or decking so extra water can be absorbed. You could use a combination of mulch and ground covers in some areas, while you could leave the lawn in place in others. If you leave the lawn, change it to a freedom lawn (see Step 5 for more details on freedom lawns).

The Ceiling

When your trees are still young, it's a good idea to create some shade with vine-covered pergolas or arbors, but be sure to control exuberant vines that might climb onto the house or other buildings. Suspending one or more triangular shade sails above your outdoor room can provide shade and unify the area. You could even create a vine-covered tepee or other shelter for the kids.

CEILING

CONTAINER & SCREENING PLANTS

WALLS

Walls

The sides of your outdoor room could be a combination of container gardens, screening plants, and/or fences. Be sure to leave enough room for your projected activities in order to avoid a closed-in feeling. On the other hand, a small outdoor room hidden from view can offer intimacy and a place to get away.

OUTDOOR ACTIVITIES

Let's look at some ideas on how to structure spaces for some typical outdoor activities. You and your family may have other ideas, so work with everyone to come up with practical solutions for your needs and wants.

Cooking and Eating

Plan for this use before you start planting, because some plants are highly flammable, such as bunching grasses, saw palmetto, wax myrtle, yaupon holly, red cedar, or inkberry. Don't locate them anywhere near the grilling area or the fire pit. It's best to have no canopy over the grilling area or fire pit, but shade would be welcome over the dining or sitting areas. For further information on flammable and less flammable plants see the Florida Extension Service's brochure "Landscaping in Florida with Fire in Mind" (http://edis.ifas.ufl.edu/fr076).

Create a stable floor that will support tables, chairs, and a grill. This could be made of pavers set into the ground. The base for the pavers could be mulched soil, lawn, ground cover plants, or several inches of gravel. The gravel base will provide better drainage, especially if you have clay soil. Whichever base you choose, there will be some maintenance to clear out fallen leaves and weeds. If the pavers are interlocking with very little space, the maintenance will be somewhat less, but water could still drain into the soil.

The floor could be made of wood or synthetic decking above the ground. This would work well for a soggy area or where you want to keep the floor height the same as the house flooring. If you include a grilling area (especially charcoal), protect the deck with a fireproof cover in that area. There will probably not be many weeds that grow up through the decking, but there might be some at the edge of the decking. You may wish to plant some type of thick low shrub or ground cover around the edge of the deck, depending on its height, to displace the weeds.

The floor could be a freedom lawn if it is solid enough to support the furniture or equipment. You may want to add individual tiles or pavers under each leg of furniture for stability and to prevent wooden furniture from rotting. The advantages to this arrangement are that you can mow the area as needed and you can move the furniture away to set up the space for some other activity.

Sitting and Relaxing

The setup for relaxing activities such as reading or talking could be similar to the setup cooking and eating as discussed above, and indeed you could use your eating area for reading or other activities, but if you are not cooking or eating, you have more flexibility. You could add a bench, a hammock, or a couple of suspended chairs. You could have an open area or a closed-in nook in a back corner. You could locate your sitting area near a water feature, next to a butterfly garden, or in a meadow area with a curving path cut with a lawn mower. Your sitting area could be under a vine-covered pergola that has a fan to circulate the air for cooling and to chase away mosquitoes.

There are no limits on what you can design for relaxing and enjoying the fruits of your labor and watching all the butterflies and birds you've invited into your landscape. Hopefully enough of your neighbors will have also converted their lawns to native areas, so you won't be subjected to the endless roar of lawn equipment.

Kids and/or Pets Playing

Many people leave some unpoisoned lawn for the play area for kids or dogs so they can run around and not get hurt. You can add structures such as a sandbox, a jungle gym, a tree house, or a swing. The equipment can change over time as needed. If you add mulch under a swing or a jungle gym, do not use shredded rubber because it can release toxins into the soil, it won't break down in the soil, and it's a fire hazard.

Each year you could build a temporary teepee or hideout by using a group of poles lashed together at the top or a hoop greenhouse frame and then planting native morning glories, pole beans, cucumbers, coral honeysuckle, or other fast-growing vines around the edge that would scramble up the poles. Or you could create a room by planting a double or triple row of mammoth sunflowers outside a circle drawn on the ground. You'd need to add compost to the area where you plant vines or sunflowers to encourage fast growth and full foliage.

Edible Gardening

Most crops require full or mostly full sun. Increasingly, people are planting vegetables in their front yards because that's where the most sun is and because it's a better use than the typical front lawn. For most of Florida, raised beds are recommended, but other than that, there are many ways to configure your garden to suit your needs. It's best to grow vegetables in the winter in Florida, but there are also some great summer crops. If you have kids, growing vegetables gives them a connection to their food that is priceless, but once you get past the initial phase of learning what works for your situation, you can also save a significant amount of money by growing your own food.

Compost used for edible gardens will need to be richer than the compost you use for native plants, so add some manure from herbivores such as chickens, goats, horses, or cows. Keep one pile of compost that includes manure for your vegetable garden and another pile without manure for your native landscaping needs.

In addition to the typical crop plants, you may wish to plant some fruit-bearing trees and shrubs to add an edible forest component to your landscape. Make sure you use only plants suited for Florida's climate. New Jersey blueberries are nice, but

Dealing with a Minor Detail

In Florida, we are blessed with weather that is often compatible with extending our living area to include outdoor spaces. Previous steps in this book have covered how to attract more wildlife to your yard with more native plantings and how to work toward making your yard into its own ecosystem that can be expanded by encouraging neighbors to do the same. Community properties can also be modified to attract more wildlife.

All this is great, except for one detail: mosquitoes.

Depending on your location in Florida, mosquitoes are usually thicker during the summer, which is our wet season. You can mitigate the mosquito population in your yard using multiple strategies, but since we want to invite other bugs to our yards, no poisons—organic or otherwise—will be recommended for our mostly native landscapes.

GET RID OF STANDING WATER

Be vigilant about getting rid of standing water in less than three days, which is the time from egg laying until the hatching of the mosquito larvae, or naiads. This includes water in saucers for your container gardens, gutters, and other places where puddles can form. As discussed in Step 2, your rain gardens should be designed so that standing water is gone within three days either by soaking into the soil or being taken up by plants. In clay soils, you might need a dry well in the center of your rain garden so the extra water is not available to mosquitoes. Note: Eggs left on moist soil can last for up to a year, until the ground is flooded again, before they hatch.

If you have still water that's not a pond, such as a water garden in a container, you could add a solar-powered circulation system with a small fountain. The system should include a filter screen, and the circulation needs to be strong enough to trap the larvae against the screen.

INSTALL WATER-BASED PREDATORS

If you have a pond, purchase some native mosquito fish. They can survive even if the pond is seasonal by going dormant in the mud during the dry season.

Dragonflies are probably the most voracious of the predators, both as naiads and as adults, but you need standing water for them to lay their eggs. Ponds make great habitat for dragonflies.

Frogs and toads need water to complete their life cycles, and, like dragonflies, they eat mosquitos as larvae and as adults.

ENCOURAGE LAND-BASED PREDATORS

Encourage mosquito predators by installing bat houses or purple martin houses. Most birds, even seed-eating birds and hummingbirds eat insects, especially when they are raising their young.

INSTALL PHYSICAL DETRIMENTS

Mosquito Traps

You can buy or make mosquito traps, but most of them attract other insects as well. On top of that the traps tend to attract the insects as part of the process, so you may end up with more mosquitoes in the area. If you use traps, remove them from the area an hour or two before your scheduled outside activities.

Citronella

You can burn citronella candles or other smoky candles to repel mosquitoes to some extent during your outdoor time.

Fans

Since mosquitoes are weak fliers, you can install fans to keep the air turbulent. The fans could be overhead fans under a pergola or oscillating floor fans aimed at your sitting areas.

Insect Repellent and Long Sleeves

You can wear long sleeves and use a DEET-based insect repellent.

REFERENCE

For further reference, go to the website of American Mosquito Control Association, a nonprofit organization (www.mosquito.org).

they won't make it here. Buy only cultivars that work in Florida. The same is true of other crops like onions and garlic—only certain varieties work in Florida. Do your research: even if you've been growing vegetables your whole life elsewhere, things are different in Florida.

Plant a butterfly garden near fruit trees and the vegetable garden because many crops need to be pollinated in order to produce fruit.

For more details on growing Florida crops, see the book *Organic Methods for Vegetable Gardening in Florida* by Ginny Stibolt and Melissa Contreras.

Gardening and Composting

Because a landscape is never finished, it's a good idea to create a work space for gardening chores such as a potting bench, a place to store gardening tools, and a place for composting where trimmings from the landscape and kitchen scraps can be deposited.

A good compost pile should be at least two feet from buildings and about three feet square and three feet high, which is enough volume to heat up. It's not necessary, but some people use pallets, cinder blocks, or other materials to create a containment area for one to three piles. Having more than one pile location makes it easier to turn. Turning is the process of mixing up the pile to aerate it and to speed up the composting process. (See the introduction for more information on building compost.)

IN THE FUTURE

The human-use areas of your property may change through the years as the landscape matures and as your family's needs change. A kids' play area may become a pond or a conversation area. When your neighbors see you reading a book in the shade of a tree with butterflies and birds keeping you company while they are mowing their high-maintenance lawns, maybe they will follow your lead and plant more natives in their landscapes, too.

Your native landscape will have a more positive effect on local ecosystems if your neighbors, local schools, local community associations, and your municipality all work to convert their lawns into native landscapes. Your yard can set the example, so take good photos before, during, and after your native landscape installation and spread the word. Give talks to local garden clubs, civic groups, master gardener groups, churches, youth groups, and other organizations that might have the opportunity to change their landscape management practices.

Work with local elementary schools to help them install some butterfly gardens to replace some of their unused lawn. Installing the garden is only the first step, so be sure to work with the school or parent teacher group to plan ahead for ongoing maintenance.

Another type of outreach is to work with your county to implement roadside meadows and wildflower corridors. They will save money on roadside mowing and provide good habitat for wildlife. The Florida Wildflower Foundation (www. flawildflowers.org) offers guidelines and sample laws to make it easy to implement this program in your county. They have experience working with many Florida counties, especially in the Panhandle, and are ready to work with you, your county, and the Department of Transportation.

*Being good stewards of our lands needs to be the driving force
for how we move into the future as a society.*

Appendix

Plant List

This is a list of plants mentioned in the book. It is divided into woody and non-woody plants and then sorted by the common name used in the book. This is not a complete list of recommended plants for Florida. Indeed, some invasives mentioned in the book are on this list. They are definitely not recommended!

Here are three of the best tools for building a list of native plants recommended for your area of Florida:

- The Florida Native Plant Society website (www.fnps.org/plants) provides lists of plants by type native to your county.
- For South Florida, the Institute for Regional Conservation website (www.regionalconservation.org) has a "Natives for Your Neighborhood" link that lists appropriate native plants by zip code.
- Gil Nelson, *Florida's Best Native Landscape Plants: 200 Readily Available Species for Homeowners and Professionals* (Gainesville: University Press of Florida, 2003). This book provides complete information for commonly available landscape native plants, including information about mature size, where to plant, and good companion plants.

See the resources listed at the end of the introduction for more references.

TREES AND SHRUBS

Australian pine (*Casuarina* spp.). Three species are found in Florida, all of which are on invasive plant list of the Florida Exotic Pest Plant Council. These plants are flowering plants, not pines. They are allelopathic, so they kill other nearby plants. They are not wind tolerant. Remove these plants from the landscape as soon as possible.

Azalea (*Rhododendron* spp.). Most azaleas planted in urban and suburban landscapes are the evergreen Asian azaleas, which are not invasive but do not provide the same ecosystem services as a native plant. Five species of azalea are native to northern and central Florida; these are highly recommended for an acid environment such as an area near pines or magnolias. Most will grow to 10 feet tall and can spread to nearly as wide. The swamp azalea (*R. viscosum*) is adapted to wetter conditions. Azaleas are butterfly host plants.

Bay cedar (*Suriana maritima*). This drought-tolerant and salt-tolerant shrub, which is native to coastal areas in Central and South Florida, can grow to twelve feet. It is a butterfly host plant.

Beautyberry (*Callicarpa americana*). This deciduous shrub produces clusters of vivid purple berries that are eaten by a wide variety of birds. It grows in full sun or in partial shade and tolerates poor soil but does better in rich somewhat acidic soils. Drought tolerant. The gracefully arching canes can reach out to more than 6 feet from the main plant.

Blueberries (*Vaccinium* spp.). Five blueberries are native to Florida and are highly recommended. All of them prefer acidic soils and full to partial sun, all attract pollinators, and all provide food for wildlife. Sparkleberry (*V. arboretum*) can grow to 25 feet, the highbush species (*V. corymbosum* and *V. stamineum*) grow to 12 feet high, and the lowbush blueberries (*V. darrowii* and *V. myrsinites*) grow to only a foot or two tall. The lowbush species are generally evergreen, while the highbush spies are deciduous. There are also cultivars for edible crops in Florida. Blueberries are butterfly host plants.

Buttonbush (*Cephalanthus occidentalis*). This moisture-loving shrub is native to most of Florida and will grow to twenty feet tall. It occurs naturally in standing water at the edges of freshwater ponds and is recommended for consistently wet habitats. Its globe-shaped flower heads attract a wide variety of pollinators. Buttonbush is a butterfly host plant.

Cabbage palms. See **Palms.**

Coontie (*Zamia integrifolia*; synonym *Z. pumila*). This is Florida's only native cycad (a primitive nonflowering plant with male and female individuals). It is a slow-growing, easy-care, and well-behaved short shrub. It can grow in full sun or deep shade and is drought tolerant and salt tolerant. It has a large tuber that has been harvested for its starchiness (its other common name is arrowroot). Coontie is a butterfly host plant.

Crapemyrtle (*Lagerstroemia indica*). This overplanted tree is native to India and other parts of Asia, but it does well in Florida. While it is not recommended as a new tree, a well-established tree offers shade and perching places for birds. It can be used to start a new grove by planting native trees and shrubs around it. When native plants grow large enough, the crapemyrtle can be girdled to make room for them.

Cypress (*Taxodium* spp.). Two species of cypress are native to most of Florida: bald cypress (*T. distichum*) and pond cypress (*T. ascendens*). These occur in moist to flooded sites that have acidic soil. These large deciduous conifers are recommended for wet sites, but bald cypress can adjust to drier sites once it is established, so it can be used in large rain gardens. Don't plant them near lawn or foot traffic areas because they tend to develop knees (gnarly, vertical root extensions) that will impede walking and mowing. Both cypress species are butterfly host plants.

Elderberry (*Sambucus nigra* subsp. *canadensis*). This native tall shrub or small tree can grow to twenty-five feet tall and will spread via rhizomes, so it tends to build thickets. The wood is weak and tends to sag or break off during storms if it is not supported by other vegetation. Its large white flower heads attract pollinators and its purple-to-black berries feed the birds. Prefers full or partial sun and damp soil that is neutral to acidic.

Fig (*Ficus* spp.). Weeping fig (*F. benjamina*) is commonly used as a dense hedge in South Florida, but it takes a lot of trimming to maintain it as a hedge because it is a full-sized tree. This book recommends hedgerows of native plants to replace hedges. Quite a few figs grow in Florida, but only the strangler fig (*F. aurea*) is native. However, even this would not be recommended for a small landscape.

Hollies (*Ilex* spp.). Fifteen species of holly are native to Florida. All do well in acidic soil and all are recommended. Hollies are dioecious with male and female plants. Only the females will bear berries. Most hollies are trees, but some are smaller trees and inkberry (*I. glabra*) is a shrub. Yaupon holly (*I. vomitoria*) has a tendency to sucker: even its popular dwarf cultivar (*I. vomitoria* 'Nana'), which is a known male clone and has no fruit, sends out suckers. Dahoon holly (*I. cassine*) grows to about forty feet tall, while East Palatka holly (*I. x attenuata* 'East Palatka'), a naturally occurring hybrid of dahoon holly and American holly (*I. opaca*), grows to about twenty-five feet tall and is known for its heavy fruit production.

Inkberry. See **Hollies**.

Jamaica caper (*Quadrella jamaicensis*). This is a tall, drought-tolerant shrub that is tolerant of salt spray. Prefers rich soil that is neutral to slightly alkaline. Recommended for South Florida, its native region. Showy white flowers attract pollinators. Jamaica caper is a butterfly host plant.

Magnolias (*Magnolia* spp.). Six species of magnolia are native to Florida, but only two are commonly sold and both are recommended: southern magnolia (*M. grandiflora*), which is native to central and northern Florida and sweetbay magnolia (*M. virginiana*), which occurs in all of Florida except for the Keys.

Both prefer neutral to acidic soils. The sweetbay magnolia is more tolerant
of wet soils and is recommended for rain gardens. It also tends to sucker to
create thickets around itself. The southern magnolia is drought tolerant and is
often used as a lawn tree despite the fact that it sheds its large, leathery leaves
throughout the year. Fragrant flowers attract pollinators and the seeds feed
birds and other wildlife. Magnolias are butterfly host plants.

Maples (*Acer* spp.). Five species of maple are native to Florida, but red maple (*A. rubrum*) is the most widespread; it occurs in all but the southernmost counties
of the state. This tree grows to seventy or more feet tall, has wide-spreading
roots, and can tolerate standing water, which makes it a good rain garden plant
if there is room for it to grow. It tends to sucker both at its base and from its
surface roots. Maples are butterfly host plants.

Marlberry (*Ardisia escallonioides*). This evergreen, shade-tolerant plant is native
to Central and South Florida. It grows as a shrub or a small tree that attracts
pollinators and birds. It occurs naturally as an understory plant, but it will
work as a screen or in a hedgerow. Do not confuse with the invasive species in
this genus, coral ardisia (*A. crenata*).

Oaks (Quercus spp.). More than twenty species of oaks are native to Florida.
Some are huge, wide spreading trees like the live oak (*Q. virginiana*) and some
are ground covers less than one foot tall such as dwarf live oak (*Q. minima*).
Oaks provide good habitat values on several levels: their acorns fed wildlife and
they host a wide variety of butterfly and moth larvae.

Oakleaf hydrangea (*Hydrangea quercifolia*). This is a large shrub that is native to
North Florida. It is recommended for hedgerows because of its coarse texture,
showy whitish flower heads, and good fall color. Prefers dry or well-drained
neutral to acidic soil.

Palms. Several palms are native to Florida. They belong to a few different genera.
Many nonnative palms are also widely planted. Some, such as the queen palm
(*Syagrus romanzoffiana*) have been shown to be invasive in Florida. Palms
serve as trees in our landscapes, but since they do not produce real wood
with annual rings, they are not true trees botanically. This is a desirable trait if
your goal is to avoid disturbing underground infrastructure: palm roots don't
expand, so they will not displace sidewalks, foundations, or other hardscape
structures in the landscape. Our state tree, the cabbage palm (*Sabal palmetto*),
spends its first decade or more in its palmetto state while it develops the girth
of its trunk. Once the girth is developed, it will then begin to grow vertically. It
is usually sold as a field-grown tree that is probably about forty to fifty years old
and has almost all of its fronds cut off. (At no other time should this palm have
such a severe pruning.) Palms have a large inflorescence that attracts many

pollinators and their fruit feeds a wide variety of wildlife. Native palms are butterfly host plants.

Palmettos. Palmettos are similar to palm trees, but they typically do not grow vertically. Most are native to Florida. Some, such as saw palmetto (*Serenoa repens*), develop trunks that lay on the ground. Palmettos are recommended for landscapes as part of a hedgerow or wild area. Like palms, they have large inflorescences that attract pollinators and their fruit is eaten by a variety of birds and other wildlife. Palmettos are butterfly host plants.

Paperbark (*Melaleuca quinquenervia*). The Florida Exotic Pest Plant Council has shown that paperbark is highly invasive in South Florida. When it is removed from an area, its wood is shredded and sold as FloriMulch. This mulch is recommended for the landscape, because the more that is sold, the more this tree will be harvested.

Pigeon plum (*Coccaloba diversifolia*). This drought-tolerant and salt-tolerant tree grows to fifty feet and is native to coast counties in South Florida. It attracts pollinators and its fruit is eaten by birds and other wildlife.

Pines (*Pinus* spp.). Seven species of pine are native to Florida. All prefer well-drained, acidic soils. They are generally fast growers, but longleaf pine (*P. palustris*) gets a slow start while it develops its especially fire-tolerant form with deep roots. Wildlife feed on the seeds.

Red cedar (*Juniperus virginiana*). Red cedar is a dioecious, medium-sized evergreen conifer that is native to most of Florida. It is a pioneer species that grows well on upland disturbed sites. It is often used as a screen and is a good addition to a hedgerow, but give it room to spread. It offers good habitat values because of its denseness and berry-like cones. Red cedar is a butterfly host plant.

Seagrape (*Coccoloba uvifera*). Seagrape is native to coastal areas in Central and South Florida. It is highly salt tolerant and drought tolerant. This fast-growing tree or shrub tends to sprawl, but it can grow to thirty-five feet tall, so give it room. Seagrape provides food and shelter for birds.

St. John's worts (*Hypericum* spp.). These are mostly short-lived shrubs with yellow flowers that can bloom through the winter, even in northern sections of the state. This long blooming season is important for butterflies and other pollinators that might break dormancy during warm spells in the winter. More than twenty varieties of St. John's worts are native to Florida, and mostly they will plant themselves in wild or untended meadows.

Strongbarks (*Bourreria* spp.). There are three species of strongbarks. All of them are native to the southernmost counties of Florida. They prefer well-drained alkaline soils. Strongbarks attract pollinators and birds.

Wax myrtle (*Morella cerifera*; synonym *Myrica cerifera*). This tall shrub or small tree is native to all of Florida. Two other native species of *Morella* occur mostly in the Panhandle. This highly adaptable, salt-tolerant, evergreen shrub grows well in poor soils because its roots fix nitrogen. It produces suckers, so plant it where that won't make a difference, but it tolerates being trimmed into a tidy hedge. Wax myrtles are dioecious, so make sure there are both male and female plants in the neighborhood so berries will be produced. The prolific waxy berries of this plant provide food for winter songbirds. It is good for screening or for hedgerows and can tolerate trimming to become a formal hedge as well. Wax myrtles are rain garden plants and butterfly host plants.

Wild coffee or Seminole balsamo (*Psychotria nervosa*). This evergreen understory shrub is native to Central and South Florida. It prefers full to partial shade and well-drained soil that is neutral to alkaline. Its attractive fruit and shiny leaves create interest in the landscape, feed the birds, and provide contrast in a hedgerow. Three other species of wild coffees are native to Florida, but *P. nervosa* is the most widespread.

Willows (*Salix* spp.). Coastal plain willow (*S. caroliniana*), a native plant, is the most common member of the genus in Florida, but a few other willows are also natives. They attract pollinators with their early flowers and are a larval host for butterflies. They are naturally found in wet sites and are a good rain garden plant, but they can adjust to drier sites. Willows are not wind tolerant. They often send up many sprouts from the base of the trunk. The roots aggressively seek water, so do not plant it anywhere near septic or sewer pipes.

HERBACEOUS PLANTS

Beach bean or baybean (*Canavalia rosea*). This legume is native to coastal areas in Central and South Florida. It is a drought-tolerant, salt-tolerant ground cover for sandy areas.

Black-eyed Susans (*Rudbeckia* spp.). *R. hirta* is the most widespread and most widely available of the nine Rudbeckia species native to Florida, but the others are also worthy additions to your landscape. It occurs naturally in meadows, roadside ditches, and other disturbed habitats. It attracts pollinators and seed-eating birds. Most black-eyed Susans are short-lived perennials, but they usually self-sow if the conditions are right. Rudbeckias are butterfly host plants. They need full sun to thrive, so annual mowing to maintain a meadow ecosystem is necessary. While they can adjust to drier conditions, they will do better with some irrigation during droughts.

Blazing stars (*Liatris* spp.). More than a dozen Liatris species are native to Florida. Most are short-lived perennials that die back each winter. They can occur naturally in wet or damp meadows or in sandy uplands. They are attractive to butterflies and other pollinators.

Blue curls (*Trichostema* spp.). Two species of blue curls are native to Florida, but forked blue curls (*T. dichotomum*) is the most common. A freely reseeding annual, it is likely to plant itself in sunny or partially sunny dry locations. Attracts pollinators, including hummingbirds.

Blue-eyed grasses (*Sisyrinchium* spp.). Four blue-eyed grasses are native to Florida, but the narrowleaf blue-eyed grass (*S. angustifolium*) is the most common and most commonly sold. This dainty member of the iris family is a bunching, short-lived perennial that has showy pale blue flowers in the spring. Use as a turfgrass substitute in a lawn, in short damp meadows, or at the edges of rain gardens. Can take mowing and light foot traffic.

Bluestem grasses (*Andropogon* spp.). These are tough bunching grasses that can grow in acidic, poor soil. Because of their bluish leaves and showy inflorescences, these natives are a great choice for a meadow or for filling in between native trees and shrubs while you're waiting for them to grow. Bluestem grasses are a butterfly host plant.

Brackens (*Pteridium* spp.). Three brackens are native to Florida, but tailed bracken (*P. aquilinum* var. *pseudocaudatum*) is the most widespread. However, you're not likely to find these for sale in the native trade. They are tough, long-lived ferns that spread via deep rhizomes and can tolerate drought and full sun.

Cardinal flower (*Lobelia cardinalis*). This short-lived perennial is native to most of Florida and is a beautiful addition to an acidic, damp, or wet garden area. Its red tubular flowers attract hummingbirds and butterflies, but it's not usually a good rain garden plant in Florida because our seven-month-long dry season will kill it unless it's irrigated.

Carolina jessamine (*Gelsemium sempervirens*). This native, fast-growing, evergreen, winter-flowering vine can be used on trellises and fences or as a ground cover in sunny and partial shade areas. Its showy flowers are also fragrant. It roots readily. Carolina jessamine is poisonous to livestock and pets. Even though it's a fast grower, it's relatively easy to control.

Chain ferns (*Woodwardia* spp.). These native ferns form colonies in wooded or partially shaded areas. While they occur naturally in wet sites, they can adapt to drier locations as long as there is some shade. Use as a ground cover in your groves once there is some shade. The netted chain fern (*W. areolata*) has stiff, fertile fronds that usually persist through the winter, but the sterile fronds die back where there is frost.

Cinnamon fern (*Osmunda cinnamomea*). This large, native, clumping fern makes quite a statement in damp or wet habitats. It will grow well in full sun if it has a reliably wet soil. If the soil dries out for part of the year, provide some shade. Cinnamon ferns are good for rain gardens that are partially shaded. The fertile frond is the color of cinnamon. In Florida, it sends up fertile fronds in the spring and the fall. Sterile fronds that appear in the spring will keep growing until late fall, when they die back.

Coral honeysuckle or trumpet honeysuckle (*Lonicera sempervirens*). This long-lived native vine provides excellent habitat values. Its beautiful red tubular flowers attract hummingbirds and butterflies and its orange berries are eaten by a wide variety of songbirds. It blooms best if it is allowed to climb a fence or trellis, but it can also serve as a ground cover. Coral honeysuckle is a butterfly host plant.

Cross vine (*Bignonia capreolata*). Cross vine occurs in the central and northern areas of Florida. This woody vine has flowers that attract hummingbirds. The woody stem has the shape of a cross. This vine is not as aggressive as other woody vines.

Fakahatchee grass or eastern gamagrass (*Tripsacum dactyloides*). This tough, large bunching grass is somewhat salt tolerant and is native to most of Florida. Use as a hedge or for edging, in foundation plantings, or as backdrop for perennial borders. Its unusual inflorescence adds interest in the landscape and offers good habitat values. Fakahatchee grass is a butterfly host plant.

False rosemary or scrub mint (*Conradina* spp.). Four false rosemaries are native to Florida. All attract pollinators. Large-flowered rosemary (*C. grandiflora*) occurs in the southeastern counties. They are drought tolerant but not salt tolerant. Plant in dry sandy locations.

Ferns. See **Brackens, Chain ferns, Cinnamon fern, Leather ferns, Royal fern,** and **Horsetail,** a fern ally.

Frog fruit or turkey tangle fogfruit (*Phyla nodiflora*). This widespread native plant grows coast to coast and in all parts of Florida. It's a great ground cover and serves well as a turfgrass substitute. You probably already have this plant growing under your feet. Frog fruit attracts pollinators and is a butterfly host plant.

Goldenrod (*Solidago* spp.). Twenty goldenrods native to Florida, but none of them has ever caused allergic reactions due to floating pollen. Because they are all pollinated by insects, their pollen is heavy and sticky. They are recommended for pollinator gardens and for meadows because they bloom from late summer into fall. They spread via rhizomes and will build colonies that show as a sea of yellow. They die back in the winter. Most prefer dry sunny habitats. Goldenrods are butterfly host plants.

Grapes (*Vitis* spp.). Several grapes are native to Florida. These woody vines are aggressive in the landscape and can cover whole trees in just a few years. Birds eat the fruit and plant them widely. Use grapes with care in the landscape, but they do offer food and shelter to wildlife.

Grasses. Bunching grasses can play important roles in the landscape, from edging meadows or serving as hedges to serving as foundation plantings or transition areas next to wooded areas. For non-turf grasses, see **Bluestem grasses, Fakahatchee grass, Muhly grass,** and **Sea oats**. For turf grass, see **St. Augustine** and **Zoysia**.

Horsetail or scouring rush (*Equisetum hyemale* var. *affine*). This native fern ally (a nonflowering, spore-producing plant) is an evergreen that loves moisture and spreads aggressively once it is established. Recommended for edges of ponds but not for rain gardens because it's not drought tolerant.

Indian blanket (*Gaillardia pulchella*). This native drought-tolerant, short-lived perennial blooms profusely even in poor sandy soils. It grows best in full sun and is often used in meadows and roadside plantings. It attracts pollinators and seed-eating birds later in the season. Recommended.

Irises (*Iris* spp.). Several species of iris are native to Florida. Most occur in the central and northern counties. Any would be recommended for wet or damp sites with full or partial sun. It will spread in favorable conditions. The two that are most available in the native plant trade are the Dixie iris (*I. hexagona*) and the blue flag iris (*I. virginica*).

Leather ferns (*Acrostichum* spp.). The native giant leather fern (*A. danaeifolium*), a bunching, evergreen fern, requires wet or moist habitats with rich soil. It will grow in most of the peninsular sections of the state, but in South Florida it can grow to eight feet tall. Golden leather fern (*A. aureum*) is also native, but it occurs mostly in southwest Florida.

Lovegrasses (*Eragrostis* spp.). A large number of lovegrass species occur in Florida, but not all of them are native, so be careful with your selection. Most do best in loamy, slightly moist soils. The stems often arch over, giving them a fountain or weeping form. Use them as edge plants to highlight this form. Lovegrass is a butterfly host plant.

Meadow beauty (*Rhexia* spp.). Several species of meadow beauty are native to Florida. They are not usually available in the native plant trade, but they are likely to plant themselves in wet meadows in partial shade. Meadow beauty attracts pollinators.

Meadow garlic (*Allium canadense*). This native, tough perennial garlic occurs naturally in damp ditches, but it can also do well in drier sites and may already exist in damp places in a freedom lawn. It has flat leaves and an unusual inflorescence that includes both bulblets and flowers on stalks. It dies back in the summer and resprouts in the late fall. Meadow garlic is a good rain garden plant.

Milkweeds (*Asclepias* spp.). About twenty milkweeds are native to Florida. They are an important addition to a native landscape because they are the only larval food for monarch and queen butterflies. Some species do well in moist habitats while others work well in dry fields, so match the species to the local conditions. Milkweeds attract butterflies and other pollinators and are butterfly host plants. Note: Scarlet or tropical milkweed (*A. curassavica*) is widely sold, but it's not native to Florida and is harmful to monarch butterflies, especially in South Florida. If you have it, cut it to the ground from December to February.

Morning glories (*Ipomoea* spp.). These plants are garden favorites for their showy flowers. Six of the two dozen species that occur in Florida are natives. Two species do well on sand dunes—beach morning-glory (*I. imperati*) and railroad vine (*I. pes-caprae*)—but most species appreciate more fertility and moisture. Butterfly host plants.

Muhly grass or hairawn muhly (*Muhlenbergia capillaris*). This easy-to-grow grass is a tough but beautiful bunching grass with pink flower heads. It is a favorite in native landscapes. It is salt tolerant and drought tolerant once it is established. Small seed-eating birds will consume the seeds. Muhly grass is a butterfly host plant. Two other Florida species, gulf hairawn muhly (*M. sericea*) and cutover muhly (*Brachyelytrum erectum*) are sometimes sold as *M. capillaris*; any of the three are good additions to the landscape.

Passionvine (*Passiflora* spp.). In most of their range these herbaceous vines die back in the winter, but in frost-free zones they are evergreen. They sprout pretty much anywhere within several yards of the original plant in the spring. Twelve species occur in the wild in Florida, but only half of them are native, so be sure that any you acquire are natives. They attract pollinators and are the larval food for several butterflies, including Florida's state butterfly, the zebra longwing (*Heliconius charithonia*).

Pickerelweed (*Pontederia cordata*). Pickerelweed is a clumping, emergent perennial with a showy purple spike of flowers that attracts pollinators. (An emergent plant is one that grows in shallow water so that its roots are underwater, but the top emerges above the water surface.) It is native to all of

Florida. It grows in acidic to neutral soil, but the soil must be wet. Pickerelweed works well by itself or with other freshwater shoreline plants. Various waterfowl eat the seeds.

Rain lily (*Zephyranthes* spp.). These bulbaceous perennials are in the amaryllis family. They occur naturally in wet meadows and ditches but can grow well in drier habitats. Three rain lilies are native to Florida, but the most abundant is the atamasco lily (*Z. atamasca*). Normally they are short lived, but colonies can last for many years in the right conditions. They tend to bloom in the spring a few days after a heavy rainfall, but by the middle of summer they will die back. The grass-like leaves are not particularly noticeable when they are not blooming. Nonnative rain lilies are frequently sold.

Rosinweed (*Silphium* spp.). Two rosinweeds are native to Florida. They occur mostly in North-Central and North Florida counties. They are members of the daisy family and have yellow flowers. Starry rosinweed (*S. asteriscus*) and kidneyleaf rosinweed (*S. compositum*) can be distinguished from each other by their leaves. Both attract pollinators and are good additions to dry meadows.

Rosemary. See **False rosemary**.

Royal fern (*Osmunda regalis* var. *spectabilis*). This magnificent large clumping fern deserves its common name. Its fronds have fully separated, doubly pinnate leaves that appear lacy. The fertile fronds appear only at the top of the main sterile fronds. Plant only in partially shady habitats that are moist to wet. It's native to all of Florida, but in the northern areas, the fronds die back in the winter.

Rushes. A number of rushes are native to Florida, but common rush (*Juncus effuses*) is the most useful in landscapes. This adaptable soft rush grows as an emergent plant, a shoreline plant, and an upland plant. It volunteers in unmanaged moist acidic areas in landscapes. It is very useful for holding shorelines and as an attractive bunching, spiky plant in all but the driest landscape. Rushes work well in rain gardens.

Sages (*Salvia* spp.). Several sages are native to Florida. They are members of the mint family and any would be recommended. Tropical sage (*S. coccinea*), an annual or short-lived perennial, is widely sold. Its beautiful tubular red flowers attract butterflies, bees, and hummingbirds. It grows in full sun or partial shade. Tropical sage grows best in poor neutral to slightly alkaline soils, but it adapts to many habitats and reseeds aggressively. Lyre-leaf sage (*S. lyrata*), a short-lived perennial, has basal leaves that stay close to the ground and a flower stalk that sports blue flowers. Lyre-leaf sage also attracts pollinators, but it tolerates mowing. They are both butterfly host plants.

Scarlet hibiscus or scarlet rosemallow (*Hibiscus coccineus*). This native wetlands perennial produces large, showy red (and sometimes white) flowers. It dies back in the winter, but if conditions are right it will increase the number of shoots each year. Seeds that are not eaten will float and plant themselves around the shoreline. A number of other hibiscus species are native to Florida; any are recommended for damp or wet areas. Scarlet hibiscus is a butterfly host plant.

Sea lavender (*Heliotropium gnaphalodes*). This long-lived perennial is native to southeast Florida. It's a beach plant is drought tolerant and salt tolerant and attracts pollinators, mostly butterflies.

Sea oats (*Uniola paniculata*). This tough native grass occurs on beaches and sand dunes. It spreads by deep rhizomes and is salt tolerant and drought tolerant. Birds eat the seeds. It is recommended for sandy coastal areas. It's protected, so purchase only from trusted native nurseries.

Sedges. A number of sedges are native to Florida and most of them prefer wet habitats. Probably the one that is most available and most desirable is white-topped sedge or starrush white-top (*Rhynchospora colorata*). This lovely small sedge naturally occurs in wet places and along shorelines and roadside ditches. It is somewhat salt tolerant. It may adapt to somewhat drier habitats if they are shady. Use in damp meadows, in a rain garden, or even as a lawn substitute in damp areas. Unlike most sedges, it is pollinated by insects; the white bracts attract the pollinators.

Spanish needles or beggarticks (*Bidens alba*). Several species of Bidens are native to Florida, but *B. alba* is by far the most widespread and the most aggressive in areas where the soil has been disturbed. It definitely needs to be knocked back in wild areas or when you are starting a meadow, but its flowers attract as many pollinators as other pollinator plants (if not more). It's best to keep it confined to specific locations in the landscape and to trim it back to reduce seed dispersal. Learn to recognize it as a seedling, so when you pull them out you can add them to a salad or a mess of greens.

Spotted beebalm (*Monarda punctata*). This tough bunching perennial, a member of the mint family, is attractive to a wide variety of pollinators. This native is tolerant of salt spray and will grow well in damp or dry soils. This is a wonderful addition to a butterfly garden or meadow.

Sunflowers (*Helianthus* spp.). At least fourteen species of sunflowers are native to Florida. Some are annuals; others are perennials. Sunflowers occur in a wide variety of habitats, from beaches, where a ground-hugging dune sunflower (*H. debilis*) decorates sand dunes of the east coast, to freshwater marshes and damp roadside ditches, where the swamp sunflower (*H. angustifolius*) makes a show in the fall. Other sunflower species are found in more neutral habitats, so make the right choice for your habitat. Sunflowers attract pollinators, seed-eating birds, and other wildlife. They are butterfly host plants.

Sunshine mimosa or powderpuff (*Mimosa strigillosa*). This beautiful native vining ground cover is evergreen in frost-free climates but tends to be deciduous in its more northerly range. It's a legume and can grow well in poor, sandy soils because its roots fix nitrogen, but it prefers a slightly acidic soil in a sunny or partial shade area. It makes a beautiful turfgrass substitute with its pink powderpuff flower heads, and it withstands light foot traffic. It's an aggressive spreader and is somewhat allopathic (it exudes an herbicide, which discourages other plants in the area.) Sunshine mimosa attracts pollinators and is a butterfly host plant.

St. Augustine grass (*Stenotaphrum secundatum*). While this spreading grass is overplanted as sod for lawns, it is actually native to Florida. It does best in moist, lightly shaded environments. Most people who build native landscapes work to remove this grass, but those who move to freedom lawns may find that some of this grass will survive even with a minimum of care.

Tickseeds (*Coreopsis* spp.). Tickseeds are meadow plants. Twelve of the fifteen species that occur in Florida are native. Most have yellow flower heads. Some are annuals and others are short-lived perennials. They are Florida's state wildflower. Most coreopsis species prefer moist, sunny habitats, but some do well in drier conditions. They attract a wide variety of pollinators. They will do well with an annual mowing in the winter.

Trumpet creeper (*Campsis radicans*). Trumpet creeper is a native wood vine that can be quite aggressive in the landscape. Its showy orange trumpet flowers attract hummingbirds and butterflies. Use with care.

Twinflower (*Dyschoriste* spp.). Three species of twinflower are native to Florida and any of them could be used as a ground cover or lawn substitute. They are short-lived perennials that die back in the winter, so it should be mixed with other ground covers. Twinflower is drought tolerant. It attracts pollinators and is a butterfly host plant.

Vines. Vines are used for many purposes in the landscape, from ground cover to screening using trellises. Herbaceous vines include passionvine and Carolina jessamine. Woody vines include cross vine, trumpet creeper, and Virginia creeper.

Virginia creeper (*Parthenocissus quinquefolia*). This native woody vine offers food and shelter for wildlife. The leaves turn red in the fall. Virginia creeper is an aggressive climber and a prolific reseeder, so use with care.

Zoysia grasses (*Zoysia* spp.). A few species of this Asian grass are often used for lawns in Florida. It turns brown in winter and during droughts. Zoysia grasses create high-maintenance lawns that need large amounts of fertilizer and irrigation to keep them green. They are not recommended for sustainable landscapes.

Index

GINNY STIBOLT, a lifelong gardener, earned a MS degree in botany at the University of Maryland. She has been writing about her adventures in Florida gardening since 2004. Since she joined the Florida Native Plant Society in 2006, she has been including more native plants and more natural areas in her yard. In addition to writing books, she manages a "Sustainable Gardening for Florida" Facebook page and writes for her own blog at www.GreenGardeningMatters.com.

MARJORIE SHROPSHIRE is a visual artist whose work is deeply concerned with the conservation of Florida's natural areas. She is an advocate of using regionally appropriate plants native to Florida in landscaping, and she edits and produces the Florida Native Plant Society's magazine *Palmetto*. Marjorie has a BFA degree in graphic design from the University of Miami, Coral Gables, Florida.

Printed in the USA
CPSIA information can be obtained
at www.ICGtesting.com
LVHW081751190324
774699LV00002B/6